Robert Cooke

**The Visitation of London in the Year 1568**

Robert Cooke

**The Visitation of London in the Year 1568**

ISBN/EAN: 9783744794091

Printed in Europe, USA, Canada, Australia, Japan

Cover: Foto ©ninafisch / pixelio.de

More available books at **www.hansebooks.com**

# THE

# PUBLICATIONS

OF

# The Harleian Society.

ESTABLISHED A.D. MDCCCLXIX.

## Volume I.

FOR THE YEAR MDCCCLXIX.

# The Visitation of London

## In the Year

## 1568.

TAKEN BY

# ROBERT COOKE,

### Clarenceux King of Arms,

AND SINCE AUGMENTED BOTH WITH DESCENTS AND ARMS.

EDITED BY

## JOSEPH JACKSON HOWARD, LL.D., F.S.A.,

AND

## GEORGE JOHN ARMYTAGE, F.S.A.

*At a Meeting of the Council of the* HARLEIAN SOCIETY, *held at 8, Danes Inn, London, W.C., on the 28th day of May,* 1869, *the Honourable* HENRY ROPER CURZON *in the Chair, it was resolved that—*

"*The First Publication of the Society be* THE HERALDIC VISITATION OF LONDON IN 1568, *by Robert Cooke, Clarenceux King of Arms, to be edited by* JOSEPH JACKSON HOWARD, ESQ., LL.D., F.S.A., *and* GEORGE JOHN ARMYTAGE, ESQ., F.S.A."

# Preface.

———

THE Visitation contained in the following pages was taken by Robert Cooke, Clarenceux King of Arms in the year 1568. The copy from which it is transcribed forms one of the Harleian Manuscripts in the British Museum. It is in the handwriting of Nicholas Charles, who died in 1613, and the additions subsequent to that date are by William Camden, Clarenceux King of Arms, who bought Charles's books at his death. It is impossible to draw the exact line between the original Visitation and the additions, but the undoubted repute in which both heralds were held who possessed it renders it unnecessary.

The Editors cannot conclude these few preliminary remarks without acknowledging their great obligation to Mr. JOHN DAVIDSON, a member of the Council of the Harleian Society, to whom the Society is indebted for the very elaborate Index appended to the Work.

JOSEPH JACKSON HOWARD.
GEORGE J. ARMYTAGE.

LONDON,
*December* 31*st*, 1869.

# List of Pedigrees.

# LIST OF PEDIGREES.

# The Visitacon of London,

TAKEN BY ROBERT COOKE, CLARENCEUX KING OF ARMES,
AN° DOM. 1568, AND SINCE AUGMENTED BOTH WITH
DESCENTS AND ARMES. (HARL. MSS., No. 1463.)

## Chester.

ARMS. *Per pale argent and sable, a chevron engrailed between three rams'-heads erased, armed or, all counterchanged, within a bordure engrailed gules bezanté.*
CREST. *A ram's-head couped argent, armed or.*

William Chester of London, gent.=

John Chester eldest sonne=Joan da. of — Hill of London.
of London, gent.

Nicholas Chester 1 filius. =

Elizabeth da. of= John Turner & widowe of Alderman Beswick.

Sᵣ William Chester Knight Mayor of London, 2 sonne, 1560, 2 Eliz. =Elizabeth d. of Tho. Lovett of Astwell in com. Northt. Ar. 1 wife.

Richard Chester now living 1568.

Arms, *Quarterly of eight :—*
1. *Argent, three wolves passant in pale sable.* (LOVETT.)
2. *Ermine, a bordure azure bezantée.* (TURVILLE.)
3. *Argent, a cross voided between four cross crosslets fitchée gules.* (BILLING.)
4. *Gules, three lions passant argent.* (GIFFORD.)
5. *Azure, two bendlets between six martlets or.* (PRAYERS.)
6. *Per pale or and azure, a chevron ermine.* (JEWELL.)
7. *Argent, a chief indented azure.* (CRAUFORD.)
8. *Argent, a cross engrailed gules.* (DRAYTON.)

Thomas 2 sonne — 3. John. — 4. Daniel. — 5. Francis.

Francisca wife to Francis Robynson of London Grocer.

Jane wife to Richard Offley, brother to Sir Tho Offley.

William Chester of London sonne and heire. =

Judith da. and coheyre of Anthony Cave of Chichley in Com. Buck. Ar.

Emme wife to John Gardener of London Grocer.

Susanna wife to John Trott of London, Draper.

Anthony Chester his only sonne and heyre.

13

# White.

ARMS. *Per fess azure and or, a pale counterchanged, upon the first three plates each charged with two bars wavy vert, on the second as many lions' heads erased gules.*
CREST. *A lion's head erased quarterly azure and or, gutté counterchanged.*

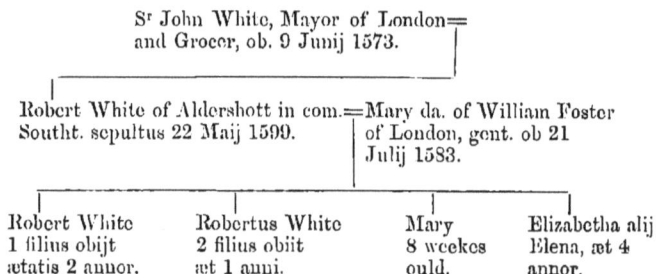

Sʳ John White, Mayor of London=
and Grocer, ob. 9 Junij 1573.

Robert White of Aldershott in com.=Mary da. of William Foster
Southt. sepultus 22 Maij 1599.       of London, gent. ob 21
                                     Julij 1583.

| Robert White 1 filius obijt ætatis 2 annor. | Robertus White 2 filius obiit æt 1 anni. | Mary 8 weekes ould. | Elizabetha alij Elena, æt 4 annor. |

---

# Martyn.

ARMS. *Quarterly :—1 and 4. Argent, a chevron between three mascles sable within a bordure engrailed gules. 2 and 3. Gules, a fess engrailed between three swans' heads erased argent (both for MARTYN).*
CREST. *A cockatrice's head or, beaked and wattled gules, between two wings expanded vert.*

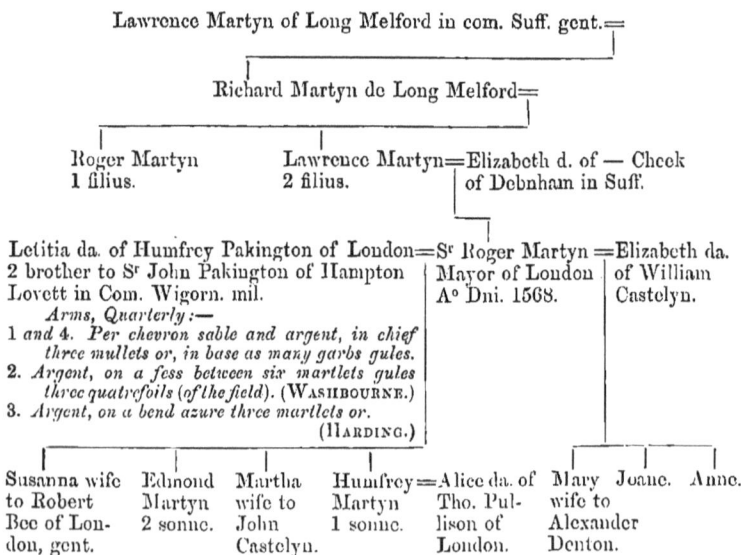

Lawrence Martyn of Long Melford in com. Suff. gent.=

Richard Martyn de Long Melford=

| Roger Martyn 1 filius. | Lawrence Martyn=Elizabeth d. of — Cheek 2 filius.        of Debnham in Suff. |

Letitia da. of Humfrey Pakington of London=Sʳ Roger Martyn =Elizabeth da.
2 brother to Sʳ John Pakington of Hampton | Mayor of London | of William
Lovett in Com. Wigorn. mil.                A° Dni. 1568.   | Castelyn.
*Arms, Quarterly :—*
1 and 4. *Per chevron sable and argent, in chief three mullets or, in base as many garbs gules.*
2. *Argent, on a fess between six martlets gules three quatrefoils (of the field).* (WASHBOURNE.)
3. *Argent, on a bend azure three martlets or.*
        (HARDING.)

| Susanna wife to Robert Bee of London, gent. | Edmond Martyn 2 sonne. | Martha wife to John Castelyn. | Humfrey Martyn 1 sonne | =Alice da. of Tho. Pullison of London. | Mary wife to Alexander Denton. | Joane. | Anne. |

# Champion.

ARMS. *Or, on a fess gules between three trefoils slipped ermines, an eagle displayed of the field within a bordure engrailed azure.*
CREST. *An arm erect couped at the elbow, habited gules, charged with three bars or, holding in the hand proper a rose-branch of the last.*

Sᵣ Richard Champion=Barbara da. of — Watson of Lidington in com.
Knight, Mayor of  Rotel gen.
London, Aº Dni 1565. ARMS. *Argent, on a chevron engrailed azure between three martlets sable as many crescents or, each charged with a torteau.*

---

# Avenon.

ARMS. *Ermine, on a pale gules a cross flory or, on a chief sable a billet of the third within a mascle between two escallops argent.*
CREST. *A parrot's head erased vert, wings expanded per pale azure and gules, double collared or, holding in his beak of the third an olive-branch of the first.*

Sᵣ Alexander Avenon Knight,=Elizabeth da. of John Slowz.
Mayor of London. | ARMS. *Or, on a fess gules between three pomies a cinquefoil pierced ermine between two martlets argent.*

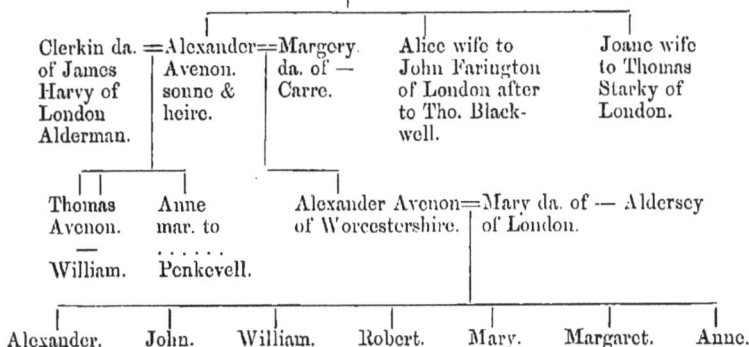

Clerkin da. =Alexander==Margery. | Alice wife to | Joane wife
of James | Avenon. | da. of — | John Farington | to Thomas
Harvy of | sonne & | Carre. | of London after | Starky of
London | heire. | | to Tho. Black- | London.
Alderman. | | | well.

Thomas | Anne | Alexander Avenon=Mary da. of — Aldersey
Avenon. | mar. to | of Worcestershire. | of London.
— | ...... |
William. | Penkevell. |

Alexander. John. William. Robert. Mary. Margaret. Anne.

# Harper.

ARMS. *Azure, on a fess between three eagles displayed or, a fret between two martlets of the first.*

CREST. *Upon a crescent or, charged with a fret between two martlets azure, an eagle displayed of the last.*

| . . . . . . . . vxor= | S$^r$ William Harper = | Alice d. of — Tom- = | Richard Harison |
|---|---|---|---|
| ejus. | Knight Maior of | linson ob. 10 Octo- | of Shropshire 1 |
| *Per chevron* | London. | ber 1569. | husband. |
| *gules and ar-* | | *Chequy or and azure,* | |
| *gent three trefoils slipped,* | | *a fess argent fretty* | |
| *counterchanged, on a chief* | | *gules bezanté.* | |
| *of the second three mart-* | | | |
| *lets of the first.* | | | |

Beatrix Harison vnica
filia, nupta — Prestwood.

# Draper.

ARMS. *Quarterly:*—1. *Argent, on a fess between three annulets gules a mullet between two covered cups or* (DRAPER). 2. *Argent, on two chevrons between three escallops sable six martlets or* (DRAPER). 3. *Ermine, on a chief azure three lions rampant or* (AUCHER). 4. *Ermine, a fess chequy sable and argent.* (URSWICK.)

CREST. *A stag's-head sable attired or, charged on the neck with two bars between three annulets of the second; a mullet for difference.*

John Draper of Flintham in com. Nottingham Ar.=

Thomas Draper= — filia et hæres Anger et vxoris ejus
of Flintham.     filiæ et heredis Vrswik.

Tho. Draper = — filia Ketleby.          Robert Draper= — da. and coheyre
of Flintham.                              2 sonne.        of — Fyfeild.

Joh'nes Draper= — filia     Mathew Draper    Benett wife to    Elizabeth wife to
               Gunstone. of Camberwell.  John Fromonde.   John Bowyer.

Thomas Draper.     William Draper.     S$^r$ Christopher Draper=Margaret da.
                                        Knight 3 sonne Mayor | of Henry
                                        of London 1566.       Greene of
                                                              Essex.

Benett wife to        Anne wife to S$^r$       Brigida wife to
William Webbe         Wolston Dixye            Stephen Woodroff
of London.            Alderman of              of London.
                      London.

# Rowe.

ARMS. *Argent, on a chevron azure between three trefoils slipped party per pale gules and vert, three bezants ; in chief a crescent for difference.*
CREST. *Gules, a stag's-head attired or, a crescent for difference.*

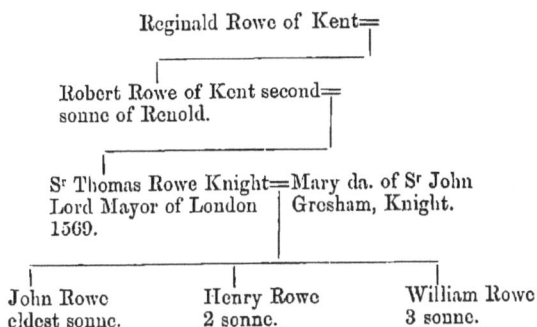

Reginald Rowe of Kent⚊

Robert Rowe of Kent second⚊
sonne of Renold.

Sᵣ Thomas Rowe Knight⚊Mary da. of Sᵣ John
Lord Mayor of London | Gresham, Knight.
1569.

| John Rowe eldest sonne. | Henry Rowe 2 sonne. | William Rowe 3 sonne. |

# Garrard.

ARMS. *Argent, on a fess sable a lion passant of the field.*
CREST. *A leopard sejant proper.*

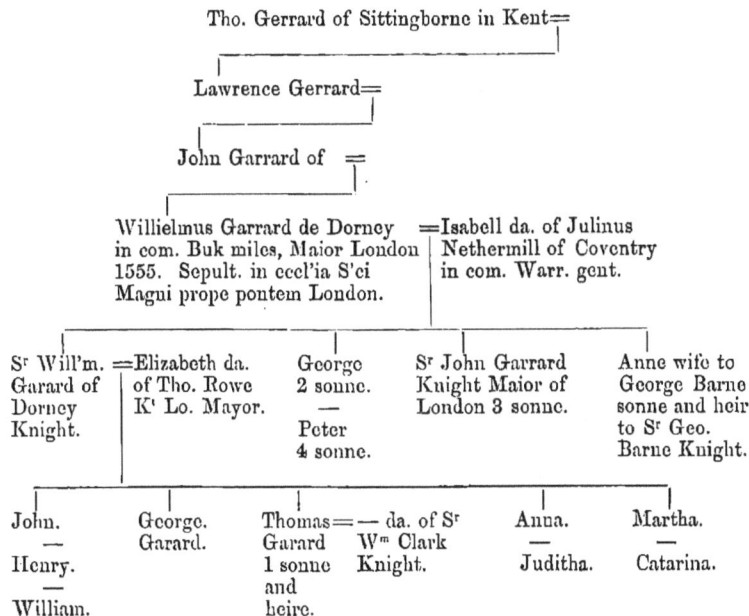

Tho. Gerrard of Sittingborne in Kent⚊

Lawrence Gerrard⚊

John Garrard of ⚊ .

Willielmus Garrard de Dorney     ⚊Isabell da. of Julinus
in com. Buk miles, Maior London | Nethermill of Coventry
1555. Sepult. in eccl'ia S'ci | in com. Warr. gent.
Magni prope pontem London.

| Sᵣ Will'm. Garard of Dorney Knight. | ⚊Elizabeth da. of Tho. Rowe Kᵗ Lo. Mayor. | George 2 sonne. — Peter 4 sonne. | Sᵣ John Garrard Knight Maior of London 3 sonne. | Anne wife to George Barne sonne and heir to Sᵣ Geo. Barne Knight. |

| John. — Henry. — William. | George. Garard. | Thomas⚊— da. of Sᵣ Garard Wᵐ Clark 1 sonne Knight. and heire. | Anna. — Juditha. | Martha. — Catarina. |

# Langley.

ARMS. *Ermine, on a bend vert three leopards' faces or.*
CREST. *A cockatrice sable, combed and wattled gules.*

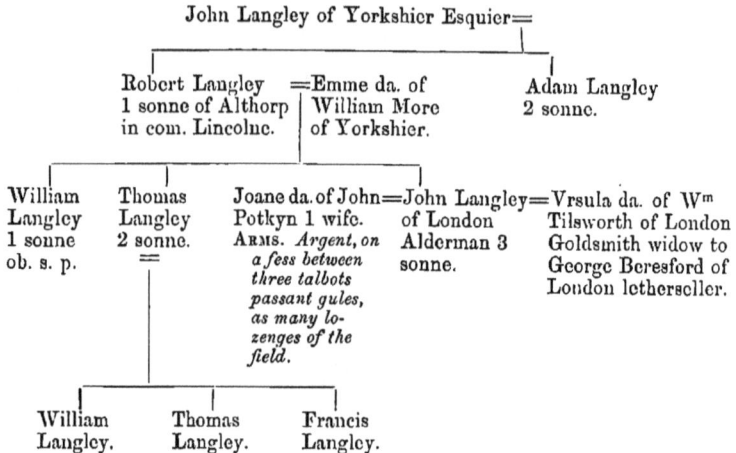

John Langley of Yorkshier Esquier⹀

Robert Langley =Emme da. of    Adam Langley
1 sonne of Althorp | William More    2 sonne.
in com. Lincolnc. | of Yorkshier.

William    Thomas    Joane da. of John=John Langley=Vrsula da. of Wᵐ
Langley    Langley    Potkyn 1 wifc.    of London    Tilsworth of London
1 sonne    2 sonne.    ARMS. *Argent, on*    Aldorman 3    Goldsmith widow to
ob. s. p.    =    *a fess between*    sonne.    George Beresford of
            *three talbots*    London letherseller.
            *passant gules,*
            *as many lo-*
            *zenges of the*
            *field.*

William    Thomas    Francis
Langley.    Langley.    Langley.

# Allen.

ARMS. *Per fesse sable and or, a pale engrailed counterchanged, on the first three*
  *talbots passant or, collared gules.*
CREST. *A talbot passant sable, collared gules, ears and chain or.*

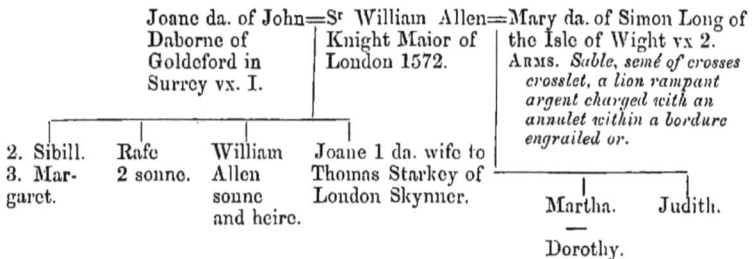

Joane da. of John=Sʳ William Allen=Mary da. of Simon Long of
Daborne of    Knight Maior of    the Isle of Wight vx 2.
Goldeford in    London 1572.    ARMS. *Sable, semé of crosses*
Surrey vx. I.        *crosslet, a lion rampant*
            *argent charged with an*
            *annulet within a bordure*
            *engrailed or.*

2. Sibill.    Rafe    William    Joane 1 da. wife to
3. Mar-    2 sonne.    Allen    Thomas Starkey of
garet.        sonne    London Skynner.
        and heire.            Martha.    Judith.

                        Dorothy.

## Duckett.

ARMS. *Quarterly* :—1. *Sable, on a saltire argent a mullet for difference.* (DUCKETT.) 2. *Gules, three cushions ermine tasseled or.* (REDMAN.) 3. *Gules, a lion rampant argent, charged with a fleur-de-lis sable, within a bordure engrailed of the second.* (ALDBOROUGH.) 4. *Gules, semée of crosses crosslet or, a saltire argent; over all a mullet sable for difference.* (WINDESORE.)
CREST. *A lavender sheaf proper, banded or.*

| Mary da. of Hugh Leighton=Sʳ Lionell Duckett=Jane da. of Humfrey Pakington | | |
|---|---|---|
| of Leighton in com. Salop. | Knight Maior of London. | Esq. vx. 2. *Arms, Quarterly :—* 1 and 4. *Per chevron sable and argent, in chief three mullets or, in base as many garbs gules.* 2. *Argent, on a fess between six martlets gules three quatrefoils.* (WASHBOURNE.) 3. *Argent, on a bend azure three martlets or.* (HARDING.) |
| George Duckett died young. | Thomas Duckett sonne and heyre. | |

## Hawes.

ARMS. *Azure, on a chevron or three cinquefoils pierced purpure, a canton ermine.*
CREST. *Out of a ducal coronet or, a stag's-head argent attired of the first.*

| Sʳ James Hawes Knight=Audrey da. of John Copwood. | | | |
|---|---|---|---|
| Maior of London. | ARMS. *Argent, a pile in bend sable fimbriated and engrailed gules between two eagles displayed vert.* | | |
| John Hawes sonne & heire. | Margaret wife to John Wattes of London, Clothworker. | Elizabeth wife to Thomas Wilford. | Mary wife to John Smith of London, Mercer. |

## Ribres.

ARMS. *Azure, a fess engrailed argent, surmounted of another gules, charged with three roses of the second.*
CREST. *Out of a bunch of reeds vert, a demi swan with wings expanded argent, ducally gorged or.*

| Sʳ John Rivers Knight Mayor of=Elizabeth da. of Sʳ George Barne of | | | | | |
|---|---|---|---|---|---|
| London (in 1573). | | London Knight. *Arms, Quarterly :—* 1 and 4. *Argent, on a chevron engrailed azure three trefoils or, between as many Cornish choughs sable.* 2 and 3. *Argent, on a fess engrailed sable a rose between two fleurs-de-lis argent between three greyhounds' heads erased sable coilared or.* | | | |
| John Rivers 2 sonne. | 3 Henry. 4 Richard. | 5 William. | George Rivers eldest. sonne | Edward 6 sonne. | 1 Alice. 2 Elizabeth. 3 Dorothy. |

# Warren.

Sᵣ Thomas White Mayor of London=Joane da. and heire=Sᵣ Rafe Warren
and founder of Saint John's College          of John Lake of          Knight twise Mayor
in Oxford, 2 husband.                         London.                  of London 1 husband.

Richard Warren Esq. =Elizabeth eldest da.          Joane maried to Sᵣ Henry Wil-
sonne and heire æt 30 of Sᵣ Roland Haward          liams al's. Cromwell of Hinchin-
Annor.               Knight Mayor of               brok in Com. Hunt. ob. 8 Octob.
                     London.                       1572. Sepult. in Sᵗ Benet Sherhog
                                                   in London.

Oliuer Cromwell          2 Rob't.          Joane
sonne and heire.        3 Henry.          a daughter.
                        4 Richard.

# Oliph.

ARMS. *Per pale and chevron or and sable, three greyhounds'-heads erased counter-
    changed, collared argent.*
CREST. *A cockatrice's head erased quarterly, argent and sable, beaked, combed, and
    wattled or.*

John Oliph of Foxgrave in= Joane da. of William Eves.
com. Kantij Ar. Alderman   ARMS. *Per pale sable and gules,*
of London.                     *a double-headed eagle displayed*
                               *within a bordure engrailed*
                               *argent.*

Joane daughter and heyre maried to
John Leigh of Addington in Surrey.

Olive Lee.          Anne.          Elizabeth.          Catherine.

Malen.              Joan.

# Beecher.

ARMS. *Vair gules and argent, on a canton or a stag's head caboshed sable.*
CREST. *A demi-lion erased argent, girded round the waist with a ducal coronet or.*

Henry Beecher of London Alderman=Alice d. of Thomas Heron
uxor ejus 2 da. Her conte was G on
a bend A betwene 6 martlets ar. a
lions head erased gules, on the top
of y° bend, p' name Gittins.

of Croydon 1 wife.
ARMS. *Quarterly:—*1. *Gules, a chevron engrailed between three herons statant argent, beaked and legged or.* 2. *Argent, two bends and in chief a cross crosslet sable.* 3. *Argent, a fess gules between three boars' heads couped sable.* 4. *Argent, a chevron engrailed gules between three bugle-horns sable.*

2. Edward Beecher.
—
3. Vane Beecher.
4. William.

Henry Beecher sonne and heyre.
—
5. Bartholmew.

Elizabeth, wife to Clement Kelk of London.

2. Mary.  3. Margaret.  4. Mabel.

---

# Bacon.

ARMS. *Quarterly:—*1 and 4. *Gules, on a chief argent two mullets sable.* 2 and 3. *Barry of six or and azure, a bend gules, over all a mullet for difference.*
CREST. *A boar passant ermine, charged with a mullet for difference.*

John Bacon of Drinkeston in com. Suff. Esq.=
descended of S<sup>r</sup> Edmond Bacon of Essex that
maried Margery da. and heyre of Quaplade.

Robert Bacon sonne=Isabell d. of John Cage of Perkenham in Suff.
and heyre.

John Bacon
2 sonne.

Thomas Bacon 1 sonne.

Mary da. of John Gardner of Grove Place in com. Buck. Esq.

=James Bacon 3 sonne Alderman of London maried to his 3 wife Anne da. of Humphry Pakington widow of Alderman Jackman.

=Margaret da. of W<sup>m</sup> Rawlins of London Grocer widow of Richard Goldston of London salter. *Per pale sable and argent, on a fess between three martlets as many crescents, all counterchanged.*

Sir Nich<sup>s</sup> Bacon K<sup>t</sup> 2 s.

Anne married to John Rivett of Bramston in com. Suff. gen.

James Bacon 1 sonne.

William Bacon 2 sonne.

c

# Dane.

ARMS. *Or, a chevron engrailed azure between three hinds passant gules.*
CREST. *A wolf statant argent.*

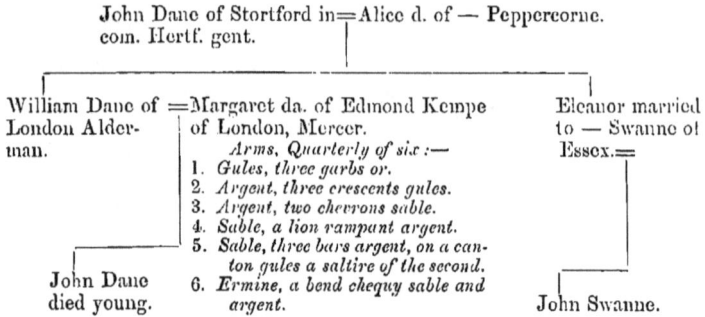

John Dane of Stortford in=Alice d. of — Peppercorne.
com. Hertf. gent.

William Dane of =Margaret da. of Edmond Kempe
London Alder-    of London, Mercer.
man.                   *Arms, Quarterly of six :—*
                1. *Gules, three garbs or.*
                2. *Argent, three crescents gules.*
                3. *Argent, two chevrons sable.*
                4. *Sable, a lion rampant argent.*
John Dane        5. *Sable, three bars argent, on a can-*
died young.           *ton gules a saltire of the second.*
                6. *Ermine, a bend chequy sable and*
                     *argent.*

Eleanor married
to — Swanne of
Essex.=

John Swanne.

# Boxe.

ARMS. *Azure, a lion passant argent, between three griffins' heads erased or.*

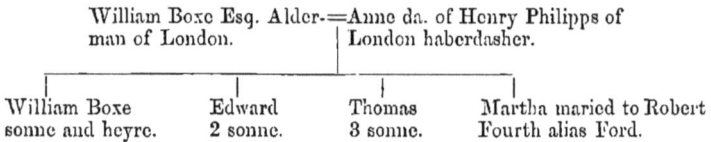

William Boxe Esq. Alder-=Anne da. of Henry Philipps of
man of London.                London haberdasher.

William Boxe        Edward        Thomas        Martha maried to Robert
sonne and heyre.    2 sonne.      3 sonne.      Fourth alias Ford.

# Pipe.

ARMS. *Azure, a fess and two bars gemelles between six cross crosslets or.*
CREST. *A demi-pegasus, wings expanded argent.*

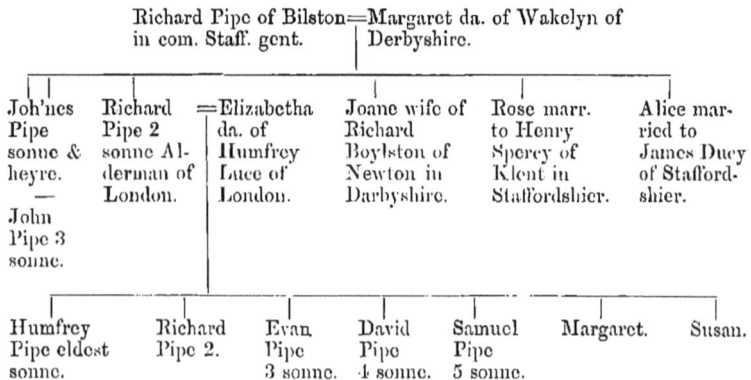

Richard Pipe of Bilston=Margaret da. of Wakelyn of
in com. Staff. gent.            Derbyshire.

Joh'nes      Richard      =Elizabetha    Joane wife of    Rose marr.    Alice mar-
Pipe         Pipe 2        da. of        Richard          to Henry      ried to
sonne &      sonne Al-     Humfrey       Boylston of      Sperey of     James Duey
heyre.       derman of     Luce of       Newton in        Klent in      of Stafford-
—            London.       London.       Darbyshire.      Staffordshier. shier.
John
Pipe 3
sonne.

Humfrey      Richard      Evan      David      Samuel      Margaret.      Susan.
Pipe eldest  Pipe 2.      Pipe      Pipe       Pipe
sonne.                    3 sonne.  4 sonne.   5 sonne.

# ꟻꟼꟷꟻꟷꟷ Myllse.

ARMS. *Quarterly :*—1 *and* 4. *Ermine, a millrind sable.* 2. *Per pale gules and azure, three lions rampant ermine.* 3. *Or, a saltire sable between four cherries within a bordure engrailed of the second.*

CREST. *A lion rampant or.*

Mylles of the Cyty of ═ — his wife d. of — Merry.
London A° D'ni 1568. ARMS. *Gules, on a fess engrailed between three water bougets erminois as many crosses pattées sable.*

# Leigh.

ARMS. *Gules, a cross engrailed argent, in the dexter chief a lozenge.*
CREST. *A unicorn's head couped or.*

— Legh ═ — d. to — Trafford.

| | | |
|---|---|---|
| Sir Thomas Leigh ═ Alice da. of John Mayor of London A° Dni 1558. | Barker al's Gery de com. Salop de Wollerton. ARMS. *Azure two bars argent, in chief a griffin's head erased or, between two pheons of the last.* | Roger. s. p. |

Will's Leigh ═ Eliz. da. of de Shawell in com. Leic. | Jo. Harper and Margaret his wife da. of John Bromley.

| | | | | | |
|---|---|---|---|---|---|
| Catharina filia Ricardi Barkley militis ux 2. | ═ Roland Leigh. | ═ Margeria da. of Tho. Lowe of London vynter. | Sir Tho. ═ Catarine, Leigh of da. of S'r Stonley Jo. Speninn com. ser of Warr. Wormleyton. | S'r Willi- ═ Frances am Leigh da. of S'r of Kinges James Newen- Haringham in ton of co. Warr. Exton Knight. Knight. | Mary mar. to Robert Andrewes of London after to Michael Cobbe. ═ |

| | |
|---|---|
| Thomas Leigh. | Elizabetha married to Hanmer of Boughton in com. Flint. |

Sir Francis ═ — da. of S'r Thomas
Leigh Egerton Lo.
Knight Chancellor of
1610. Englaud.

Alex'r Cobbe & Thomasin Cobbe. | Elizabeth Andrewes wife of Anthony Bartellett Counsellor at Law. ═

| | | | |
|---|---|---|---|
| Richard Leigh 2 sonne ob. s. p. | Winifride maried to S'r George Bond Mayor of London. ═ | Catarine mar. to Edward Barber, Sergeant at Lawe of Somersetshire. ═ | Alice wife of Tho. Cony of com. Lincolnear. ═ |

William Bond sonne & heyre. | Francis Baber. | Thomas Cony.

John Bartlett sonne & heyre. | Mary maried to Thomas Powell. ═

Anthony Powell.

# 𝕲𝖆𝖔𝖉𝖗𝖔𝖋𝖋.

ARMS. *Quarterly :—1 and 4. Gules, on a chevron (argent) three bucks' heads erased (sable), a chief per fess nebulée (sable and argent). 2 and 3. Sable, a fess ermine between two lions passant guardant argent.*

CREST. *A dexter arm embowed, habited with leaves vert, holding in the hand a branch of honeysuckle, all proper.*

David Wodroff of London  =Elizabeth da. of John Hill
Esq. and Sherif of the same | of London gent.
City 1554.

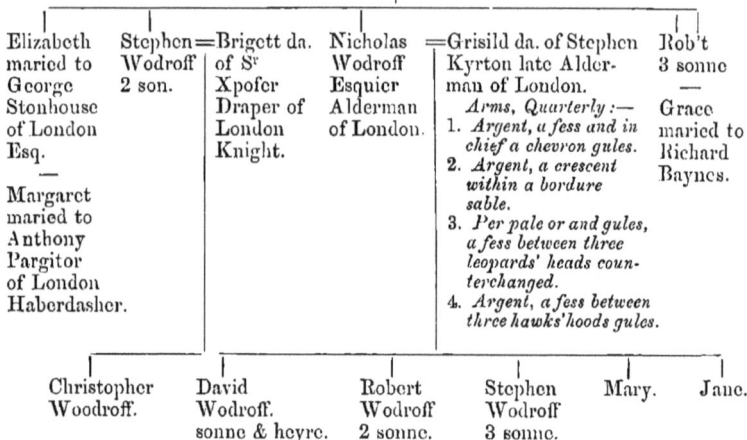

| Elizabeth maried to George Stonhouse of London Esq. —— Margaret maried to Anthony Pargitor of London Haberdasher. | Stephen=Brigett da. Wodroff | of S<sup>r</sup> 2 son. | Xpofer Draper of London Knight. | Nicholas Wodroff Esquier Alderman of London. | =Grisild da. of Stephen Kyrton late Alderman of London. |
|---|---|---|---|---|

Arms, *Quarterly :—*
1. *Argent, a fess and in chief a chevron gules.*
2. *Argent, a crescent within a bordure sable.*
3. *Per pale or and gules, a fess between three leopards' heads counterchanged.*
4. *Argent, a fess between three hawks' hoods gules.*

Rob't
3 sonne
——
Grace
maried to
Richard
Baynes.

Christopher
Woodroff.

David
Wodroff.
sonne & heyre.

Robert
Wodroff
2 sonne.

Stephen
Wodroff
3 sonne.

Mary.

Jane.

---

# 𝕭𝖑𝖆𝖓𝖈𝖐.

ARMS. *Per fess sable and ermine a pale counterchanged, on the first three demi-lions rampant or.*

CREST. *A dragon's head couped vert, collared and chained argent, holding in the mouth a firebrand of the last flamed proper.*

Thomas Blanck of Guilford in the County of Surr. gent.=

Thomas Blanck of London.=

S<sup>r</sup> Thomas Blanck Knight Lord=Margaret da. to Richard Traves
Maior of London obijt s. p.    Marchantaylor London ob. s. p.
ARMS. *Argent, a saltire between four butterflies volant sable.*

# Harvy.

ARMS. *Or, on a chevron between three leopards' heads gules a crescent of the field.*
CREST. *A leopard passant argent spotted sable, ducally gorged and chained or, re-flexed over back.*

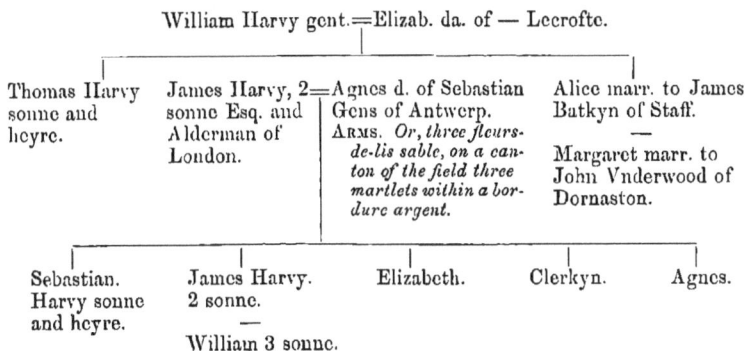

William Harvy gent.=Elizab. da. of — Lecrofte.

| Thomas Harvy sonne and heyre. | James Harvy, 2=Agnes d. of Sebastian sonne Esq. and ┃ Gens of Antwerp. Alderman of ┃ ARMS. *Or, three fleurs-* London. ┃ *de-lis sable, on a can-* ┃ *ton of the field three* ┃ *martlets within a bor-* ┃ *dure argent.* | Alice marr. to James Batkyn of Staff. — Margaret marr. to John Vnderwood of Dornaston. |

| Sebastian. Harvy sonne and heyre. | James Harvy. 2 sonne. — William 3 sonne. | Elizabeth. | Clerkyn. | Agnes. |

# Branche.

ARMS. *Quarterly:—1 and 4. Argent, a lion rampant gules, debruised by a bendlet sable. 2 and 3. Gules, a fess vair, in chief an unicorn passant between two mullets or.* (WILKINSON.)
CREST. *Out of a ducal coronet or a cockatrice's head azure beaked or, combed and wattled gules.*

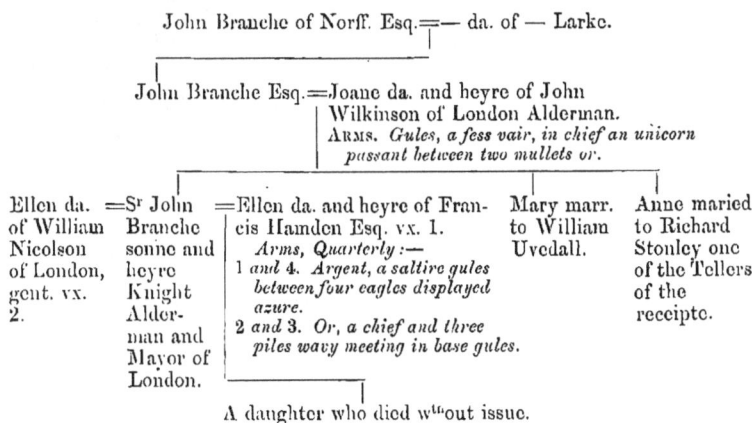

John Branche of Norff. Esq.=— da. of — Larke.

John Branche Esq.=Joane da. and heyre of John
　　　　　　　　 ┃ Wilkinson of London Alderman.
　　　　　　　　 ┃ ARMS. *Gules, a fess vair, in chief an unicorn*
　　　　　　　　 ┃ *passant between two mullets or.*

| Ellen da. =Sr John of William Branche Nicolson sonne and of London, heyre gent. vx. Knight 2. Alder-man and Mayor of London. | =Ellen da. and heyre of Fran-cis Hamden Esq. vx. 1. *Arms, Quarterly:—* 1 *and* 4. *Argent, a saltire gules between four eagles displayed azure.* 2 *and* 3. *Or, a chief and three piles wavy meeting in base gules.* | Mary marr. to William Uvedall. | Anne maried to Richard Stonley one of the Tellers of the receipte. |

A daughter who died w<sup>th</sup>out issue.

## Gamage.

ARMS. *Quarterly :—1 and 4. Argent, a bend lozengy gules, on a chief azure three escallops or. 2 and 3. Gules fretty vair.* (HORNE.)

John Gamage of Coytiff in the County of Glamorgan gent.=

William Gamage his sonne and heyre =Thomasin da. and coheyre of Edw.
of Wesenham in com. Norff. Gent.      │  Horne of Wesenham in Norff.

Anthony Gamage Esq. Alderman=Alice da. of — Symonds of
of London.                  │ Redinge.
                            │  ARMS. *Per p ile or and gules,*
                            │     *two vols paleways counterchanged.*

William Gamage sonne and heyre.

## Sebright.

ARMS. *Quarterly :—1 and 4. Argent, three cinquefoils sable. 2. Azure, six bezants, three, two, and one.* (BYSETT.) *3. Or, a saltire gules surmounted by a fess sable.* (ASHE.)
CREST. *An heraldic tiger sejant argent, tufted and ducally crowned or.*

Edward Sebright of Blakeshall in the County of Worcetor gent as apeareth most manifestly vpon the deliberate view and p'vsing of sundry very fayre and auntient deedes, charters and records of great credit and authority is lineally descended of the body of Peter Sebright of Sebrights hall in the County of Essex Esq. w^ch Peter also descended of the body of S^r Walter Sebright of Sebrightes hall Knight who lyued in the tyme of the reigne of King Henry the second, W^ch name and family of the Sebrightes as evidently apeareth by most auncient recordes beareth *Silver 3 Cinquefoyles sable pierced of the field,* And also as most evidently apeareth by a most fayre and auncient deede bearing date at Sebrightes hall the Towesday next after the feast of S^t John Baptist in the 22 yeare of the raigne of King Edward the first the sayd S^r Walter did lineally descend of the body of One of the heyres generall of Manserus Bysett a Baron sewer to King Henry the first, w^ch Manserus Bisett I do fynde as well by the auncient recordes of my Office as by the sight of an ould deede, made by the said Manserus and sealed with his Seale of Armes did beare *Azure 6 besantes gould,* And I do also fynde by view of another auncient deede that in the reigne of King Henry the second William Sebright of Sebrightes hall married Elizabeth the daughter and sole heyre of Sir Henry de Ashe Knight w^ch S^r Henry I do also fynde by the said auncient recordes did beare, *Gould a saltier goules a fess Sables.*

# Osborne.

ARMS. *Quarterly :—1 and 4. Quarterly ermine and azure, a cross or.* 2. *Argent, two bars gules, on a quarter of the second a cross of the first; in chief a crescent of the last for difference.* 3. *Argent, a chevron vert between three annulets gules.*
CREST. *An heraldic tiger passant or, tufted and maned sable, charged with an ogress.*

Sᵣ Edward Osborne Knight Cloth- =— his wife daughter of — Hewett.
worker & Mayor of London. ARMS. *Azure, on a fess flory counterflory between three lions passant argent as many lapwings proper.*

---

# Gresham.

ARMS. *Argent, a chevron ermine between three mullets pierced sable.*
CREST. *On a mound a grasshopper vert.*

John Gresham of Gresham in com. Norff.=

James Gresham of Hoult=Margery da. of William Billingford
in Norff. | of Blackford in Norff.

John Gresham sonne & heyre.=Alice da. of — Blythe. William Gresham
2 sonne.

Sᵣ John Gresham | Sᵣ Richard=Audrey da. | 1 William Gresham | Margery
4 sonne and he | Gresham | of — Lynne | Eldest sonne died | maried
maried Mary da. | Kᵗ 2 | of North- | without heyres male. | to —
& heyre of Ipswell. | sonne. | amptonshier. | — | King of
= | | | Thomas Gresham | London.
| | | a preist 3 sonne. |

Mary wife to Sᵣ Tho. | William | Edmond | Sᵣ John | Sᵣ Thomas Gresham
Rowe of London. | Gresham | Gresham | Gresham | Knight 2 sonne A
— | 1 sonne. | 3 sonne | eldest | gent of Flandres for
Vrsula maried to | — | mercer of | sonne | the Queenes Matʸ
Thomas Leveson. | John | London. | Knight. | and founder of the
— | 2 sonne. | = | = | royall exchange in
Cecily maried to | | Joane | Frances | London.
German Syoll. | | eldest | da. of — |
| | da. of | Thwaytes | =
Ellen maried to William | | Augustin | of York- | Anne da. of Willm
Vuedall of Hampshier. | | Hynde | shire. | Fernley of West
— | | Alderman | | Creting in Suff.
Elizabeth maried to | | of London. | | ARMS. *Or, on a bend*
John Elyott. | | | | *vert three stags' heads caboshed argent.*

Richard Gresham Anne. | Elizabeth maried to Sᵣ | Richard Gresham his only
sonne & heyre. | Henry Nevill Knight. | sonne who died young.

# Dyxye.

ARMS. *Quarterly :—1 and 4. Azure, a lion rampant and a chief or.* 2 and 3. *Argent, a saltire engrailed between four escallops sable.*
CREST. *A lynx sejant argent, ducally gorged or.*

Sᵣ Wolston Dyxye=Anna daughter of Sᵣ Xpofer Draper of London,
Knight Maior of          Knight and Mayor.
London died                    *Arms, Quarterly :—*
wᵗʰout issue           1. *Argent, on a fess between three annulets gules a mullet*
Aᵒ Dⁿⁱ 1593.                *argent between two covered cups or.* (DRAPER.)
                       2. *Argent, on two chevrons between three escallops sable*
                            *six martlets or.* (DRAPER.)
                       3. *Ermine, on a chief azure three lions rampant or.*
                            (AUCHER.)
                       4. *Ermine, a fess chequy sable and argent.* (ENSWICK.)

---

# Cosworth.

ARMS. *Argent, on a chevron between three falcons' wings azure five bezants.*
CREST. *A wyvern's head couped azure, purfled or, langued gules.*

John Cosworth of Cosworth in the County of Cornwall.=

John Cosworth sonne & heyre.=

John Cosworth sonne & heyre.=

Symon Cosworth sonne & heyre of John.=

Robert Cosworth sonne &=— da. of John Wolvedon of
heyre of Simon.          Woluedon in Cornwall.

Nicholas =        John Cosworth Esq. 2 sonne Mercer =Dorothy da. of Sᵣ
Cosworth          of London for that he lived after the  William Lock of
eldest             death of his nephew John is heyre    London Alderman.
sonne.             masle to the howse of Cosworth.      ARMS. *Per fess azure*
                                                         *and or, a pale coun-*
                                                         *terchanged, on the*
                                                         *first three falcons*
                                                         *rising, holding in*
                                                         *their beaks a padlock*
                                                         *of the second.*

Catarine his da. &   John Cosworth.   Thomas Cosworth   Nicholas Cosworth
heyre maried to        =              sonne and heyre.   4 sonne.
John Arundell of     Elizabeth da. of      —                 —
Trerise in Cornwall. Okinhorne.        John Cosworth 2.  William Cosworth
                                            —             5 sonne.
                                       Edward Cosworth 3 sonne.

## Egerton.

ARMS. *Quarterly :*—1. *Sable, a chevron between three pheons argent.* 2. *Ermine, a fess gules, fretty or.* 3. *Argent, a chevron between three water-bougets sable.* 4. *Vert, a chevron between three talbots passant argent.*
CREST. *A stag's head erased or.*

William Egerton Esq. descended of a younger=— daughter of — Welbeck
howse of Egerton of Wrinehill in Cheshier. | of London.

| William Egerton 1 sonne. | Thomas Egerton=Anne da. of — Langton of Hartfordshire | Mercer of who was of the howse of Langton of London. Yorkshier. |
|---|---|

ARMS. *Argent, three chevrons gules.*

| Timothy Egerton eldest sonne. | Lionell Egerton 2 sonne. | Thomas Egerton 3 sonne. | Randall. 4. Stephen. 5. Arthur. 6. | Mary 1 da. maried to John Wedgwood. | Anne 2 daughter. |
|---|---|---|---|---|---|

## Isham.

ARMS. *Gules, three piles wavy meeting in base or, over all a fess of the second.*
ANOTHER. *Gules, three piles wavy, meeting in the fess point, and a fess wavy argent.*
CREST. *A demi-swan wings endorsed argent, gutté de larmes.*

William Isham of Pitesley=Ellen da. of — Vere of
descended as heyre male of | Adington in com.
the howse of Isham in | p'dict Esq.
com. Northampton.

Ewseby Isham sonne and heyre=Anne da. of Giles Powlton of
of William. | Desborow in com. Northt. gent.

| Giles Isham= 1 sonne. | Robert a clerk 2 sonne | Gregory 3 sonne late of London Marchaunt and since of Bramstone in the county of Northampton. | John Isham 4=Eliz. da. sonne of Lamportal's.Langport in com. Northampton Esq. and also Mercer of London. | of Nicholas Barker of London. | Henry 5 sonne controller for the Custome inwards to Queene Eliz. |
|---|---|---|---|---|---|

Anne.
—
Jane.
—
Margery.

Ewseby Isham
only sonne and
heyre.

Thomas Isham 1 sonne.

Henry 2.
—
Richard 3.
—
Robert 4.

Anne 1 da. Elizabeth 2

D

# Walkeden.

ARMS. *Argent, a chevron engrailed between three griffins' heads erased azure, on a chief of the last an anchor or between two bezants.*
CREST. *A griffin's head erased quarterly argent and vert, beaked, ducally gorged, and ears or.*

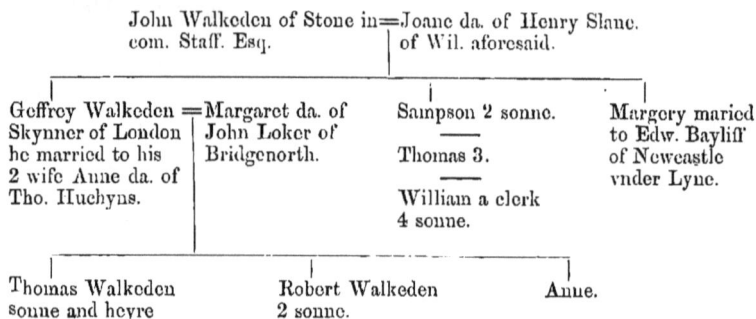

John Walkeden of Stone in=Joane da. of Henry Slane.
com. Staff. Esq. | of Wil. aforesaid.

Geffrey Walkeden =Margaret da. of
Skynner of London | John Loker of
he married to his | Bridgenorth.
2 wife Anne da. of
Tho. Huchyns.

Sampson 2 sonne.
———
Thomas 3.
———
William a clerk
4 sonne.

Margery maried
to Edw. Bayliff
of Newcastle
vnder Lyne.

Thomas Walkeden
sonne and heyre

Robert Walkeden
2 sonne.

Anne.

# Harding.

[ARMS. *Argent, on a bend azure three martlets or, on a sinister canton of the second a rose or, between two fleurs-de-lis of the field.*
CREST. *A demi-antelope proper, horned or, holding in his paws an anchor reversed.*]

=Robert Harding Alderman & Sheriff of London had 2 wifes.=

# Leveson.

ARMS. *Quarterly:—1 and 4. Azure, a fess nebulé argent and sable, between three leaves or. 2 and 3. Argent, a chevron gules between three cinquefoils pierced sable.*
CREST. *A goat's head erased argent, attired or.*

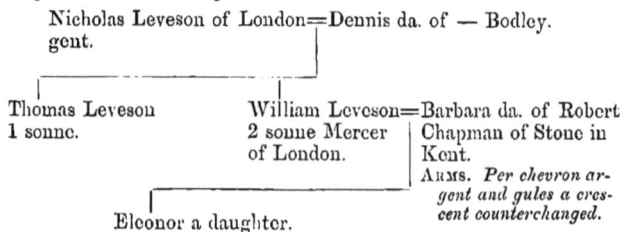

Nicholas Leveson of London=Dennis da. of — Bodley.
gent.

Thomas Leveson
1 sonne.

William Leveson=Barbara da. of Robert
2 sonne Mercer | Chapman of Stone in
of London. | Kent.
| ARMS. *Per chevron argent and gules a crescent counterchanged.*

Eleonor a daughter.

# Lowen.

ARMS. *Quarterly :—1 and 4. Quarterly per fess embattled or and azure, three stags' heads caboshed counterchanged.* 2 *and* 3. *Per chevron flory counterflory argent and gules, three martlets counterchanged.*

CREST. *A stag statant quarterly, per pale indented or and azure, the sinister horn of the first, the dexter of the last.*

John Lowen of Gerpins=Joane da. of John Plommer
al's. Gerboviles Esq. | of London Draper.

| John Lowen=Sibill da. of Sr Wil- | Thomas | Margery 1 da. | Elizabeth first |
|---|---|---|---|
| 1 sonne<br>Draper of<br>London. | liam Allen of London<br>Knight.<br>ARMS. *Per fess sable<br>and or, a pale en-<br>grailed counter-<br>changed, on the first<br>three talbots passant<br>sable, collared gules.* | Lowen<br>2 sonne. | maried to<br>John Howe<br>of London. | maried to<br>Thomas Mayatt<br>and after to<br>Wm Sherington<br>of London<br>Haberdasher. |

---

# Rivett.

ARMS. *Quarterly :—1 and 4. Argent, three bars sable, in chief as many trivets of the last.* 2 *and* 3. *Per pale argent and sable, on a chevron between three lozenges, as many martlets, all counterchanged.*

CREST. *An arm erect, couped at the elbow, per pale argent and sable, cuffed per pale of the second and first, holding in the hand proper a sword broken of the first, the handle of the second, hilt and pommel or.*

Thomas Rivett of Stow Markett=Joane da. — Raven of Needom
in Suff. Esq. | in Suff.

| James<br>Rivett<br>1 sonne<br>ARMS. 1 *and* 4.<br>*Sable on a cross en-<br>grailed between four<br>eagles displayed ar-<br>gent, five lions pas-<br>sant of the field.* 2<br>*and* 3. *Two bars<br>and on a canton gules<br>a cinquefoil or.* | Grisild da.=Thomas Rivett<br>of Willm<br>Lord Pagett. | 2 sonne of Chip-<br>penham Cam-<br>brigeshier, also<br>Citizen & Mercer<br>of London who<br>fined for his<br>shrivalty 1566. | =Alice eldest da.<br>of Sr John<br>Cotton of<br>Landwade in<br>Cambridgeshier<br>his 1 wife. | John<br>Rivett<br>3 sonne.<br>—<br>William<br>Rivett<br>4 sonne. | Miraboll<br>maried to<br>Wm Birde<br>of Lon-<br>don. |

Mirabell 1 da.     Alice 2 da.

# Browne.

ARMS. *Quarterly :—1 and 4. Argent, a chevron between three cranes sable. 2 and 3.
Sable, semé of crosses pattée fitchée, a lion rampant or.*
CREST. *An heraldic tiger azure, tufted or.*

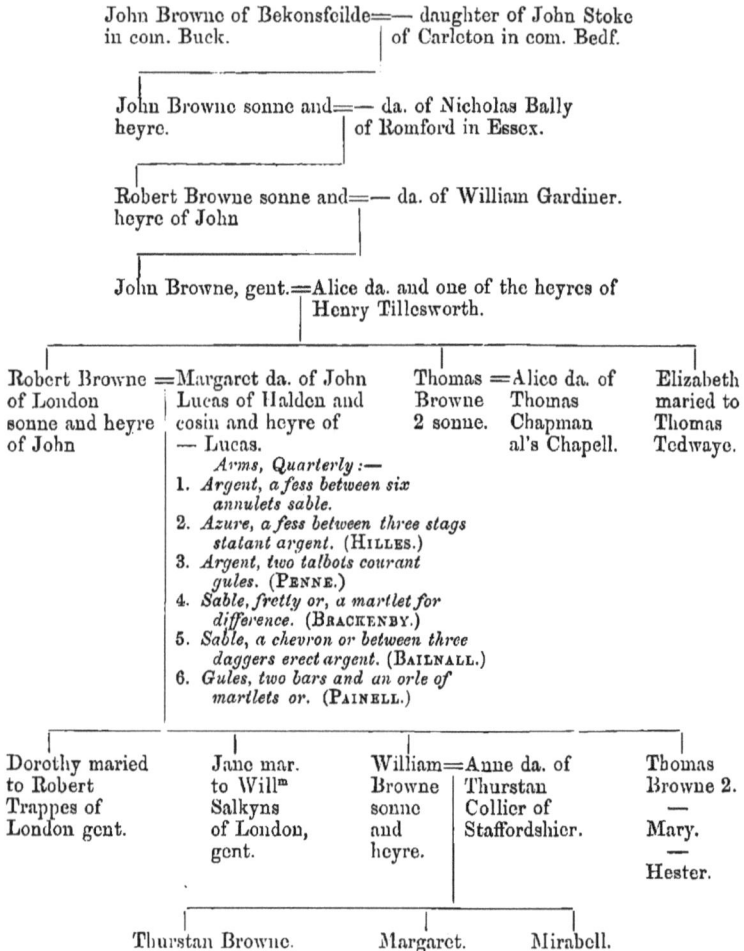

John Browne of Bekonsfeilde══— daughter of John Stoke
in com. Buck.              │ of Carleton in com. Bedf.

John Browne sonne and══— da. of Nicholas Bally
heyre.                    │ of Romford in Essex.

Robert Browne sonne and══— da. of William Gardiner.
heyre of John             │

John Browne, gent.═Alice da. and one of the heyres of
                    │ Henry Tillesworth.

Robert Browne ═Margaret da. of John        Thomas ═Alice da. of      Elizabeth
of London      Lucas of Halden and         Browne   Thomas           maried to
sonne and heyre  cosin and heyre of        2 sonne. Chapman          Thomas
of John        — Lucas.                             al's Chapell.     Tedwaye.
               *Arms, Quarterly :—*
               1. *Argent, a fess between six
                  annulets sable.*
               2. *Azure, a fess between three stags
                  statant argent.* (HILLES.)
               3. *Argent, two talbots courant
                  gules.* (PENNE.)
               4. *Sable, fretty or, a martlet for
                  difference.* (BRACKENBY.)
               5. *Sable, a chevron or between three
                  daggers erect argent.* (BAILNALL.)
               6. *Gules, two bars and an orle of
                  martlets or.* (PAINELL.)

Dorothy maried   Jane mar.        William═Anne da. of    Thomas
to Robert        to Will^m        Browne   Thurstan      Browne 2.
Trappes of       Salkyns          sonne    Collier of    —
London gent.     of London,       and      Staffordshier. Mary.
                 gent.            heyre.                  —
                                                          Hester.

Thurstan Browne.        Margaret.        Mirabell.

## Smyth.

ARMS. *Or, on a chief sable a lion passant of the first.*
CREST. *An heraldic tiger ermine, maned and tufted or.*

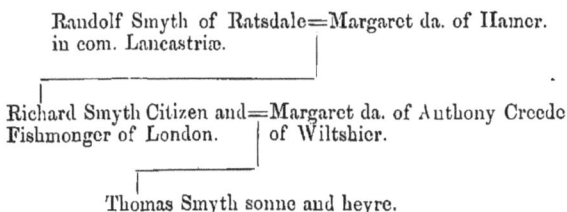

Randolf Smyth of Ratsdale=Margaret da. of Hamer.
in com. Lancastriæ.

Richard Smyth Citizen and=Margaret da. of Anthony Creede
Fishmonger of London. | of Wiltshier.

Thomas Smyth sonne and heyre.

---

## Trappes.

ARMS. *Quarterly :—1 and 4. Argent, three caltraps sable. 2 and 3. Azure, a chevron between three crosses pattée or.*
CREST. *A man's head couped at the shoulders, attired gules, garnished or, on the head a steel helmet, all proper, surmounted by a plume of three feathers argent.*

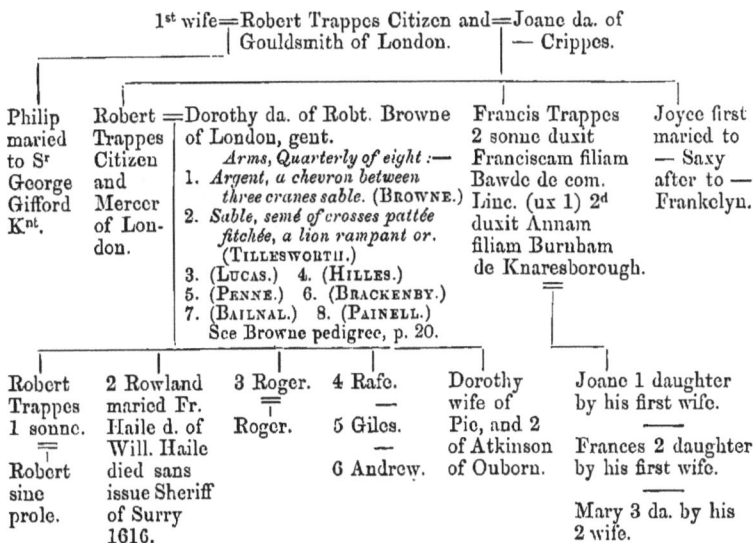

1st wife=Robert Trappes Citizen and=Joane da. of
| Gouldsmith of London. | — Crippes.

Philip
maried
to Sr
George
Gifford
Knt.

Robert =Dorothy da. of Robt. Browne
Trappes | of London, gent.
Citizen | *Arms, Quarterly of eight :—*
and | 1. *Argent, a chevron between*
Mercer | *three cranes sable.* (BROWNE.)
of Lon- | 2. *Sable, semé of crosses pattée*
don. | *fitchée, a lion rampant or.*
| (TILLESWORTH.)
| 3. (LUCAS.) 4. (HILLES.)
| 5. (PENNE.) 6. (BRACKENBY.)
| 7. (BAILNAL.) 8. (PAINELL.)
| See Browne pedigree, p. 20.

Francis Trappes
2 sonne duxit
Franciscam filiam
Bawde de com.
Line. (ux 1) 2d
duxit Annam
filiam Burnham
de Knaresborough.

Joyce first
maried to
— Saxy
after to —
Frankelyn.

Robert
Trappes
1 sonne.
Robert
sine
prole.

2 Rowland
maried Fr.
Haile d. of
Will. Haile
died sans
issue Sheriff
of Surry
1616.

3 Roger.

Roger.

4 Rafe.
—
5 Giles.
—
6 Andrew.

Dorothy
wife of
Pie, and 2
of Atkinson
of Ouborn.

Joane 1 daughter
by his first wife.

Frances 2 daughter
by his first wife.

Mary 3 da. by his
2 wife.

# Salkyns.

ARMS. *Quarterly :—1 and 4. Or, two bars between three martlets sable. 2 and 3.*
*Gules, a chevron argent, between three trefoils slipped ermine.*
CREST. *A lynx, sable.*

Stephen Salkyns of Canterbury=Joane da. of Thomas Rigdon of
in com. Cantij. gent.             Kent.

Thomas Salkyns =Agnes da. of Richard Meade of Buckingham and of his
sonne and heyre. | wife da. of Nicholas Fowntayne of Buckingham.

William Salkyns 1 sonne=Jane da. of Robert Browne of        Mary maried to
marchantaylor of             London gent.                    Henry Osmond
London.                      *Arms, Quarterly of eight :—*    of Vplumnon in
                             1. *Argent, a chevron between three*  Devonshier and
                                *cranes sable.* (BROWNE.)     had issue Agnes
                             2. *Sable, semé of crosses pattée fitché,*  and Hester.
                                *a lion rampant or.* (TILLESWORTH.)
                             3. (LUCAS.)  4. (HILLES.)
                             5. (PENNE.)  6. (BRACKENBY.)
                             7. (BAILNAL.)  8. (PAINELL.)
                             See Browne Pedigree, p. 20.

Robert Salkyns    2 John.      Margaret.        Agnes.   Hester.   filius
1 sonne.          —            —                                   s. p.
                  3 Thomas.    Vrsula.

# Dod.

ARMS. *Argent, on a fess gules between two cotises wavy sable three crescents or.*
CREST. *A serpent azure, issuing from and piercing a garb argent.*

David Dod of Edge in com. Cestr.=Catarine da. of Nicholas Manley
                                | of Powlton.

| Anne | John | Bartholmew=Elizabeth | Francis | Philip =Eliz. | William. |
|---|---|---|---|---|---|
| 1 da. | Dodd | Dod 4 sonne | da. of | 5 sonne | Dodd | da. of | 8 sonne. |
| — | 2 sonne | Haber- | George | citizen | 7 sonne | John | — |
| Elizabeth | — | dasher of | Dalton of | & haber- | citizen | Van- | Roger |
| 2 da. | David | London. | London | dash^r of | & haber- | boult | 6 sonne. |
| — | 3 sonne. | | Goldsmith. | London | dasher | of Ant- | — |
| Randolf | | | *Arms. Azure,* | maried | of Lon- | werp. | Jane |
| Dod | | | *semée of* | Mary | don. | | 3 da. |
| sonne and | | | *crosses* | da. of | | | — |
| heyre. | | | *crosslet ar-* | George | | David Dodd. | Catarine |
| | | | *gent, a lion* | Dalton | | | 4 da. |
| | | | *rampant* | of London | | | |
| | | | *guardant* | gouldsmth. | | | |
| | | | *of the last.* | | | | |

Thomas Dodd  Elizabeth.
1 sonne.     —
—            Martha.
Bartholmew   —        George Dodd   2 Nathaniel.   3 Edmond.   Catarine.
2 sonne.     Susan.   1 sonne.

# Fairfax.

ARMS. *Argent, a lion rampant sable, surmounted by three bars gemelles gules.*
CREST. *A lion's head erased sable, charged with three bars gemelles and a mullet in chief or.*

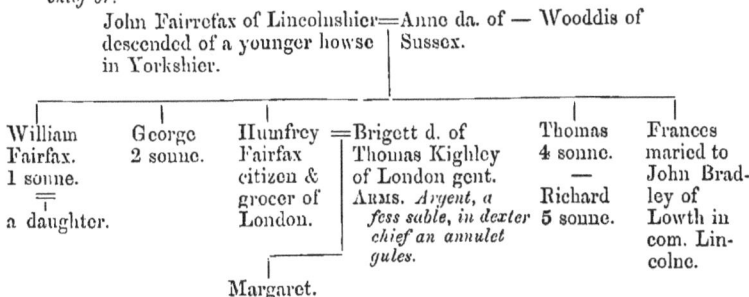

John Fairrefax of Lincolnshier=Anne da. of — Wooddis of
descended of a younger howse | Sussex.
in Yorkshier.

| William Fairfax. 1 sonne. ⹀ a daughter. | George 2 sonne. | Humfrey Fairfax citizen & grocer of London. | =Brigett d. of Thomas Kighley of London gent. ARMS. *Argent, a fess sable, in dexter chief an annulet gules.* | Thomas 4 sonne. — Richard 5 sonne. | Frances maried to John Bradley of Lowth in com. Lincolne. |

Margaret.

═════════════

# Le Taylor.

ARMS. *Quarterly :—1 and 4. Sable, a lion passant argent. 2. Or, a lion rampant guardant gules, collared argent. 3. Argent, a chevron gules between three eagles displayed sable.*
CREST. *A lynx proper.*

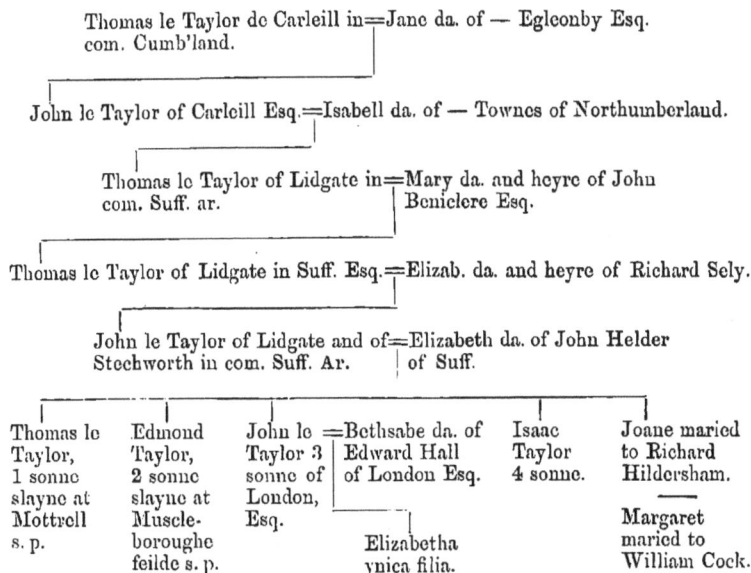

Thomas le Taylor de Carleill in=Jane da. of — Egleonby Esq.
com. Cumb'land.

John le Taylor of Carleill Esq.=Isabell da. of — Townes of Northumberland.

Thomas le Taylor of Lidgate in=Mary da. and heyre of John
com. Suff. ar. | Beniclere Esq.

Thomas le Taylor of Lidgate in Suff. Esq.=Elizab. da. and heyre of Richard Sely.

John le Taylor of Lidgate and of=Elizabeth da. of John Helder
Stechworth in com. Suff. Ar. | of Suff.

| Thomas le Taylor, 1 sonne slayne at Mottrell s. p. | Edmond Taylor, 2 sonne slayne at Muscleboroughe feilde s. p. | John le Taylor 3 sonne of London, Esq. | =Bethsabe da. of Edward Hall of London Esq. | Isaac Taylor 4 sonne. | Joane maried to Richard Hildersham. |

Elizabetha vnica filia.

Margaret maried to William Cock.

## Browne.

ARMS. *Azure, on a chevron between three escallops or, within a bordure engrailed gules a crescent of the last.*

CREST. *A crane statant azure, beaked gules, winged and collared or, charged on the breast with a crescent of the last.*

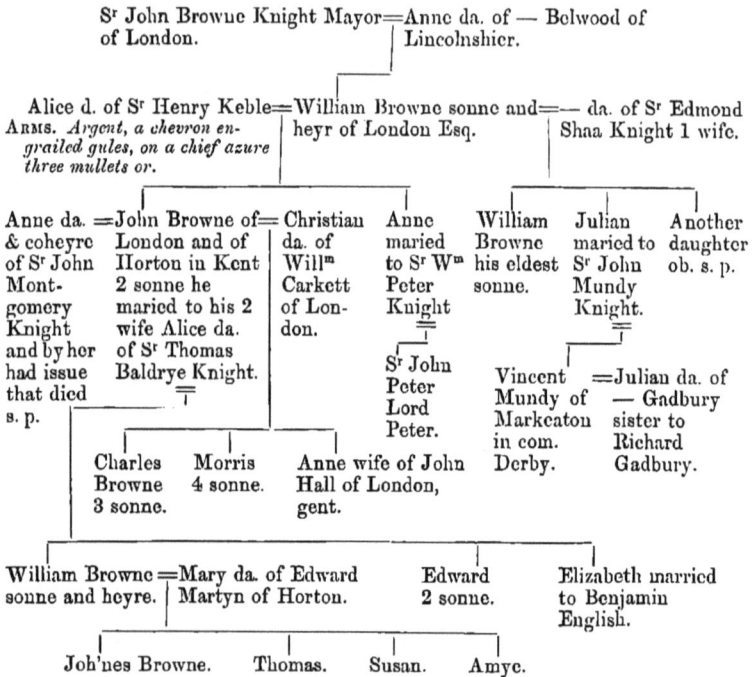

S<sup>r</sup> John Browne Knight Mayor=Anne da. of — Belwood of
of London. | Lincolnshier.

Alice d. of S<sup>r</sup> Henry Keble=William Browne sonne and=— da. of S<sup>r</sup> Edmond
ARMS. *Argent, a chevron en-* | heyr of London Esq. | Shaa Knight 1 wife.
*grailed gules, on a chief azure*
*three mullets or.*

Anne da. =John Browne of= Christian    Anne        William   Julian      Another
& coheyre  London and of   da. of       maried      Browne    maried to   daughter
of S<sup>r</sup> John  Horton in Kent   Will<sup>m</sup>     to S<sup>r</sup> W<sup>m</sup>    his eldest  S<sup>r</sup> John    ob. s. p.
Mont-      2 sonne he     Carkett      Peter       sonne.    Mundy
gomery     maried to his 2  of Lon-     Knight.                Knight.
Knight     wife Alice da.   don.                                ===
and by her  of S<sup>r</sup> Thomas                   ===
had issue  Baldrye Knight.               S<sup>r</sup> John       Vincent   =Julian da. of
that died   ===                          Peter       Mundy of   — Gadbury
s. p.                                    Lord        Markeaton  sister to
                                         Peter.      in com.    Richard
           Charles    Morris   Anne wife of John     Derby.     Gadbury.
           Browne     4 sonne. Hall of London,
           3 sonne.           gent.

William Browne =Mary da. of Edward     Edward        Elizabeth married
sonne and heyre. | Martyn of Horton.   2 sonne.      to Benjamin
                                                      English.

Joh'nes Browne.    Thomas.    Susan.    Amye.

# Barne.

ARMS. *Quarterly :—1 and 4. Azure, three leopards' heads argent. 2 and 3. Argent, a chevron azure between three Cornish choughs sable.*
CREST. *On a mound vert an eagle rising argent, beaked and ducally gorged or.*

Sir George Barne of London, Knight=Alice da. of Brooke of Shropshire.

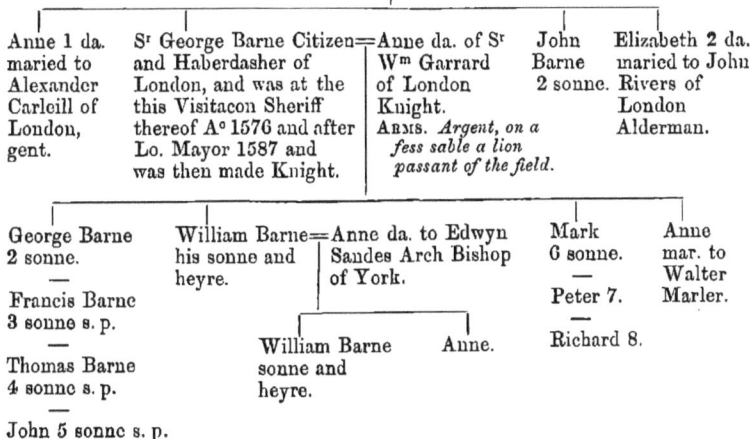

| Anne 1 da. maried to Alexander Carleill of London, gent. | Sᵣ George Barne Citizen and Haberdasher of London, and was at the this Visitacon Sheriff thereof Aᵒ 1576 and after Lo. Mayor 1587 and was then made Knight. =Anne da. of Sᵣ Wᵐ Garrard of London Knight. ARMS. *Argent, on a fess sable a lion passant of the field.* | John Barne 2 sonne. | Elizabeth 2 da. maried to John Rivers of London Alderman. |

| George Barne 2 sonne. — Francis Barne 3 sonne s. p. — Thomas Barne 4 sonne s. p. — John 5 sonne s. p. | William Barne=Anne da. to Edwyn his sonne and heyre. Sandes Arch Bishop of York. | Mark 6 sonne. — Peter 7. — Richard 8. | Anne mar. to Walter Marler. |

William Barne sonne and heyre.            Anne.

---

# Browne.

ARMS. *Or, a chevron engrailed barry wavy argent and azure, between three cranes statant of the last.*
CREST. *A crane statant azure, beaked and legged or, holding in his mouth an ear of barley of the last.*

Thomas Browne of Sᵗ Edmondsbury=Alice his wife.
in Suff. Esqᵣ.

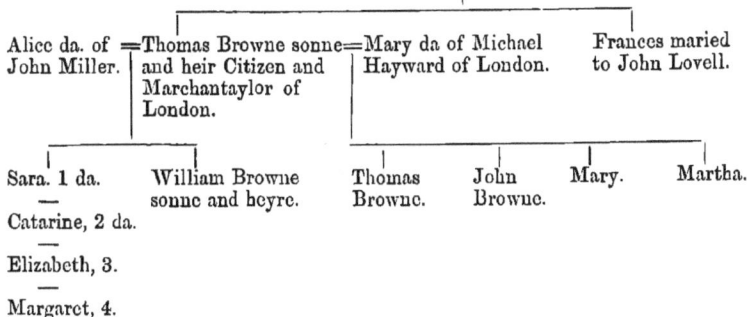

| Alice da. of John Miller. =Thomas Browne sonne and heir Citizen and Marchantaylor of London. =Mary da of Michael Hayward of London. | Frances maried to John Lovell. |

| Sara. 1 da. — Catarine, 2 da. Elizabeth, 3. Margaret, 4. | William Browne sonne and heyre. | Thomas Browne. | John Browne. | Mary. | Martha. |

E

# Lambert.

ARMS. *Argent, on a bend engrailed between two lions rampant sable, three annulets argent.*

CREST. *A demi-pegasus ermine, with wings expanded ermines.*

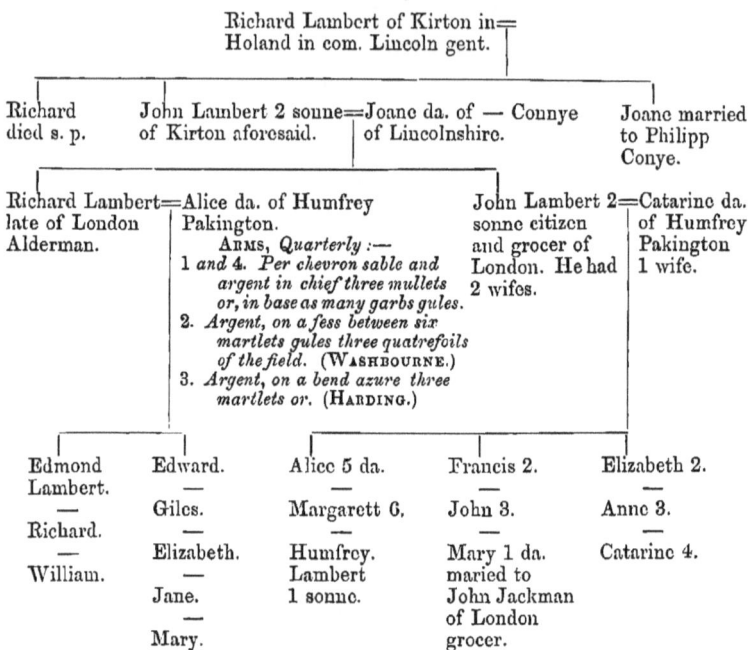

Richard Lambert of Kirton in=
Holand in com. Lincoln gent.

| Richard died s. p. | John Lambert 2 sonne=Joane da. of — Connye of Kirton aforesaid. of Lincolnshire. | Joane married to Philipp Conye. |
|---|---|---|

Richard Lambert=Alice da. of Humfrey
late of London Pakington.
Alderman.

ARMS, *Quarterly* :—
1 and 4. *Per chevron sable and argent in chief three mullets or, in base as many garbs gules.*
2. *Argent, on a fess between six martlets gules three quatrefoils of the field.* (WASHBOURNE.)
3. *Argent, on a bend azure three martlets or.* (HARDING.)

John Lambert 2=Catarine da.
sonne citizen of Humfrey
and grocer of Pakington
London. He had 1 wife.
2 wifes.

| Edmond Lambert. — Richard. — William. | Edward. — Giles. — Elizabeth. Jane. — Mary. | Alice 5 da. — Margarett 6. — Humfrey. Lambert 1 sonne. | Francis 2. — John 3. — Mary 1 da. maried to John Jackman of London grocer. | Elizabeth 2. — Anne 3. — Catarine 4. |
|---|---|---|---|---|

# Hewes.

ARMS. *Argent, on a bend sable three fish naiant of the field, fins and tails or, in chief a mullet gules.*

CREST. *An elephant's head couped azure bezanté, eared and crowned argent, charged with a mullet or.*

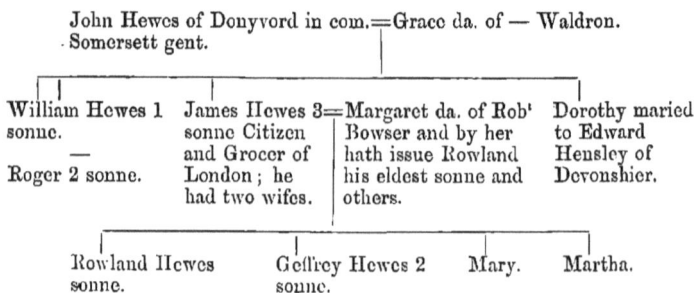

John Hewes of Donyvord in com.=Grace da. of — Waldron.
Somersett gent.

| William Hewes 1 sonne. — Roger 2 sonne. | James Hewes 3=Margaret da. of Rob^t sonne Citizen Bowser and by her and Grocer of hath issue Rowland London ; he his eldest sonne and had two wifes. others. | Dorothy maried to Edward Hensley of Devonshier. |
|---|---|---|

| Rowland Hewes sonne. | Geffrey Hewes 2 sonne. | Mary. | Martha. |
|---|---|---|---|

# Rich.

ARMS *Azure, a chevron or between two lions passant argent.*
CREST. *Out of a ducal coronet argent, a demi-lion issuant, tail forked ermine.*

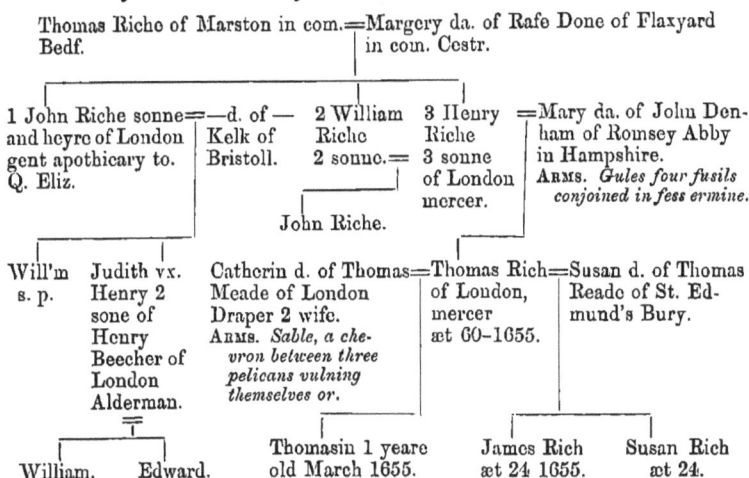

Thomas Riche of Marston in com.═Margery da. of Rafe Done of Flaxyard
Bedf. │ in com. Cestr.

1 John Riche sonne═─d. of ─  2 William  3 Henry  ═Mary da. of John Den-
and heyre of London │ Kelk of  Riche  Riche  │ ham of Romsey Abby
gent apothicary to. │ Bristoll.  2 sonne.═  3 sonne  in Hampshire.
Q. Eliz. │ of London  ARMS. *Gules four fusils*
│ │ mercer.  *conjoined in fess ermine.*
│ John Riche.

Will'm  Judith vx.  Catherin d. of Thomas═Thomas Rich═Susan d. of Thomas
s. p.  Henry 2  Meade of London  of London,  Reade of St. Ed-
│ sone of  Draper 2 wife.  mercer  mund's Bury.
│ Henry  ARMS. *Sable, a che-*  æt 60-1655.
│ Beecher of  *vron between three*
│ London  *pelicans vulning*
│ Alderman.  *themselves or.*
│ ═

William.  Edward.  Thomasin 1 yeare  James Rich  Susan Rich
│ │ old March 1655.  æt 24 1655.  æt 24.

# Stoddard.

ARMS. *Sable, three estoiles within a bordure argent.*

William Stoddard of London gent.═Emme da. ─ Cheeseman.

George Stoddard sonne and heyre═Anne da. of Henry Herdson of
Citizen of London. │ London Esq. renupta ─ Barker.
│ ARMS. *Argent, a cross sable between four*
│ *fleurs-de-lis gules.*

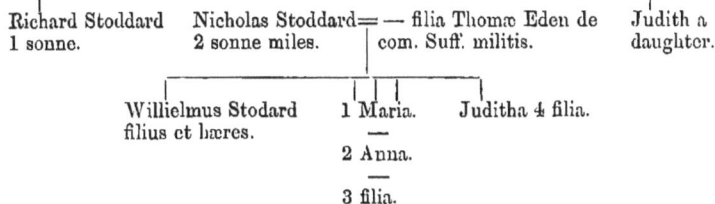

Richard Stoddard  Nicholas Stoddard═ ─ filia Thomæ Eden de  Judith a
1 sonne.  2 sonne miles. │ com. Suff. militis.  daughter.

Willielmus Stodard  1 Maria.  Juditha 4 filia.
filius et hæres.  ─
  2 Anna.

  3 filia.

# Philipps.

ARMS. *Or, a lion rampant and a chief sable.*
CREST. *A leopard sejant or.*

Thomas Philipps of Tamworth in com. Warr. gen.=Alice da. of Henry Averell.

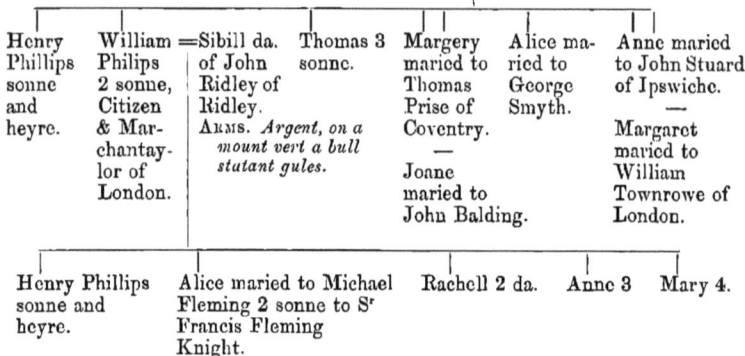

| Henry Phillips sonne and heyre. | William Philips 2 sonne, Citizen & Marchantaylor of London. | =Sibill da. of John Ridley of Ridley. ARMS. *Argent, on a mount vert a bull statant gules.* | Thomas 3 sonne. | Margery maried to Thomas Prise of Coventry. — Joane maried to John Balding. | Alice maried to George Smyth. | Anne maried to John Stuard of Ipswiche. — Margaret maried to William Townrowe of London. |
|---|---|---|---|---|---|---|

| Henry Phillips sonne and heyre. | Alice maried to Michael Fleming 2 sonne to S$^r$ Francis Fleming Knight. | Rachell 2 da. | Anne 3 | Mary 4. |
|---|---|---|---|---|

---

# Blount.

ARMS. *Quarterly :—1 and 4. Barry nebuly of six, or and sable. 2 and 3. Argent, a lion rampant gules crowned or, within a bordure engrailed sable bezanté, over all a mullet gules.*
CREST. *A lion passant gules crowned or, charged on the breast with a mullet of the last.*

William Blount of Wadeley and Glase=Joyce da. of John Pakington
in com. Salop. | of Shropshier.

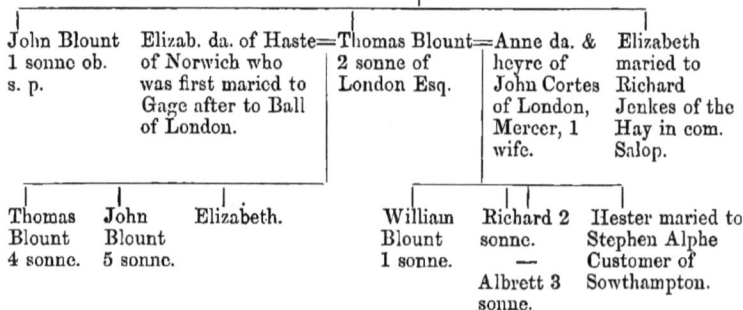

| John Blount 1 sonne ob. s. p. | Elizab. da. of Haste of Norwich who was first maried to Gage after to Ball of London. | =Thomas Blount 2 sonne of London Esq. | =Anne da. & heyre of John Cortes of London, Mercer, 1 wife. | Elizabeth maried to Richard Jenkes of the Hay in com. Salop. |
|---|---|---|---|---|

| Thomas Blount 4 sonne. | John Blount 5 sonne. | Elizabeth. | William Blount 1 sonne. | Richard 2 sonne. — Albrett 3 sonne. | Hester maried to Stephen Alphe Customer of Sowthampton. |
|---|---|---|---|---|---|

# Bowes.

ARMS. *Ermine, three bows bent in pale gules, stringed or, in chief a fleur-de-lis sable for difference.*

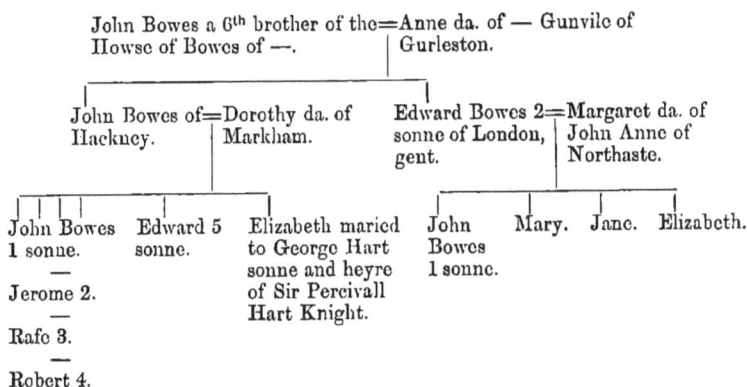

John Bowes a 6th brother of the=Anne da. of — Gunvile of
Howse of Bowes of —.     Gurleston.

John Bowes of=Dorothy da. of     Edward Bowes 2=Margaret da. of
Hackney.     Markham.     sonne of London,   John Anne of
    gent.     Northaste.

John Bowes   Edward 5   Elizabeth maried   John    Mary.   Jane.   Elizabeth.
1 sonne.    sonne.    to George Hart   Bowes
—              sonne and heyre   1 sonne.
Jerome 2.          of Sir Percivall
—              Hart Knight.
Rafe 3.
—
Robert 4.

# Hill.

ARMS. *Sable, a fess ermine between two mountain cats passant guardant argent.*

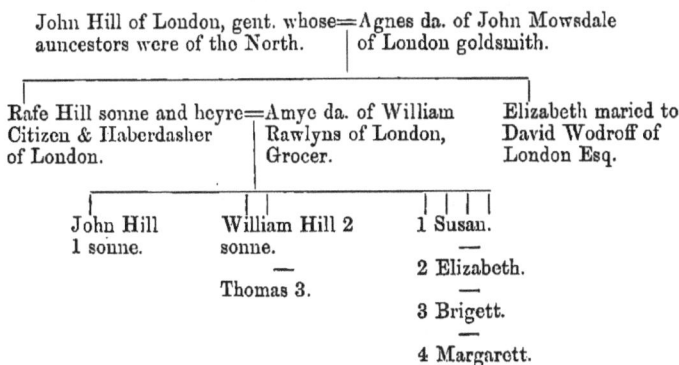

John Hill of London, gent. whose=Agnes da. of John Mowsdale
auncestors were of the North.   of London goldsmith.

Rafe Hill sonne and heyre=Amye da. of William     Elizabeth maried to
Citizen & Haberdasher   Rawlyns of London,     David Wodroff of
of London.     Grocer.     London Esq.

John Hill    William Hill 2    1 Susan.
1 sonne.    sonne.           —
           —            2 Elizabeth.
           Thomas 3.      —
                      3 Brigett.
                      —
                      4 Margarett.

# Kempe.

ARMS. *Quarterly:—Gules and argent, in the first and last quarters three garbs within a bordure engrailed or, over all a martlet sable for difference.*

Bartholomew Kempe of Gissing in Norff.═— da. of Baron Allen of Bury.

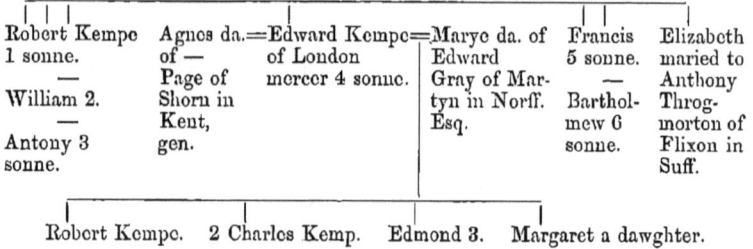

| Robert Kempe 1 sonne. — William 2. — Antony 3 sonne. | Agnes da.═ of — Page of Shorn in Kent, gen. | Edward Kempe═ of London mercer 4 sonne. | Marye da. of Edward Gray of Martyn in Norff. Esq. | Francis 5 sonne. — Barthol- mew 6 sonne. | Elizabeth maried to Anthony Throg- morton of Flixon in Suff. |

Robert Kempe.    2 Charles Kemp.    Edmond 3.    Margaret a dawghter.

# Staper.

ARMS. *Argent, a cross voided between four estoilles sable.*
CREST. *A lion sejant guardant argent, holding in his paw an estoile sable.*

Richard Staper of London,═Dionise da. of Thomas Hewett
gent.      of London, gent.

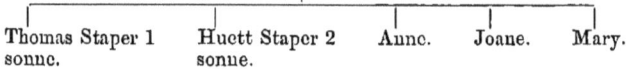

| Thomas Staper 1 sonne. | Huett Staper 2 sonne. | Anne. | Joane. | Mary. |

# Biston.

ARMS. *Sable on a bend between six crosses crosslet fitché or, a mullet of the field surmounted by a fleur-de-lis of the second for difference.*

Robert Biston of Bolton in com. Lincoln.═

2 wife da. of — ═Adam Biston his sonne & heire of ═ Agnes his 1 wife ob.
     London.      s. p.

Cutbert Biston his sonne and heyre by his 2 wife was═Alice da. of — Lacke of
Citizen and Girdler of London: he maried to his first   Northamptonshire and as
wife Joane da. of — Stanbridge by whom he had no   yet hath no issue.
issue.

# Beckett.

ARMS. *Quarterly :—*1. *Or, on a chevron between three lions' heads erased gules, a fleur-de-lis between two annulets of the field.* 2. *Argent, on a fess engrailed gules three crosses crosslet or.* 3. *Per pale sable and argent, a cross moline counterchanged.* 4. *Argent, a fess gules between three stags' heads caboshed sable, over all a crescent for difference.*

Anselme Beckett, Citizen and Haber-=Anne da. of George Dalton,
dasher of London. gent.
ARMS. *Azure semé of crosses crosslet a lion rampant guardant argent.*

William Beckett his sonne and heyre.   Judith.   Sara.   Martha.

# Burton.

ARMS. *Argent, on a chevron engrailed between three boars' heads couped sable a bezant.*
CREST. *A boar's head couped or, holding in its mouth a branch vert.*

John Burton of Stapleforth in com. Nott. gent. descended=
of a younger brother of Burton in Yorkshire.

Edmond Burton sonne & heyre Citizen and=Dionise daughter of John Knighton.
Clothworker of London. ARMS. *Quarterly :—*1 *and* 4. *Barry of eight argent and azure, on a canton gules a tun paleways or.* 2 *and* 3. *Argent, six annulets—three, two, and one—gules.*

Humphrey Burton   James 2   3 Edmond.   4 John.   Anne.   Vrsula.   Mary.
1 sonne & heyre.   sonne.

# Pierson.

ARMS. *Per fess embattled gules and azure, three suns in their splendour or.*
CREST. *A parrot vert, beaked and legged gules.*

Thomas Pierson of Barking in Essex.= — da. of John Brooke of Ilforde.

Thomas Pierson of London=Joane da. of Mathew   Joane maried to John
gent.   Gwynne of Wyndesore.   Frith of Essex.

Joh'nes Pierson   Edward 2   Mary maried to John   Elizabeth.   Philip. a da.
sonne & heyre.   sonne.   Chilestor of London
goldsmith.

# Colston.

ARMS. *Quarterly :—1 and 4. Argent, two dolphins haurient respecting each other sable, chained together by their necks, the chain pendent or. 2 and 3. Or, a lion rampant double-queued gules.*

Robert Colston of Corby in Com.=Catarine da. & coheyre of John Maloryc
Lincoln.　　　　　　　　　　　　　　of Walton in Leicestershier.

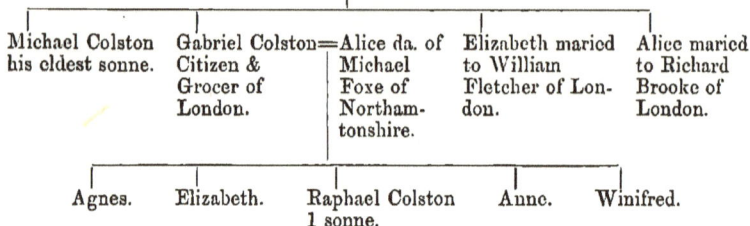

| Michael Colston his eldest sonne. | Gabriel Colston= Citizen & Grocer of London. | Alice da. of Michael Foxe of Northamtonshire. | Elizabeth maried to William Fletcher of London. | Alice maried to Richard Brooke of London. |

| Agnes. | Elizabeth. | Raphael Colston 1 sonne. | Anne. | Winifred. |

# Aldersey.

ARMS. *Gules, on a bend engrailed between two cinquefoils pierced argent three leopards' heads vert.*

Thomas Aldersey Citizen and Haberdasher=Alice da. of Richard Calthrop.
of London.

# Hogan.

ARMS. *Argent, a chevron engrailed vairy or and gules between three hurts, each charged with a lion's paw erased in bend of the field ; in chief an annulet sable.*
CREST. *A lion's paw couped and erect argent, charged with an annulet sable, holding in its claws another erased gules.*

Robert Hogan of East Bradnam in=Brigitt da. of Sʳ Richard Fowler
com. Northampt.　　　　　　　　　　of Ricott in com. Oxon.

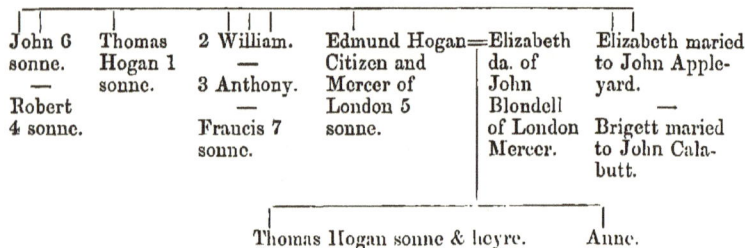

| John 6 sonne. — Robert 4 sonne. | Thomas Hogan 1 sonne. | 2 William. — 3 Anthony. — Francis 7 sonne. | Edmund Hogan= Citizen and Mercer of London 5 sonne. | Elizabeth da. of John Blondell of London Mercer. | Elizabeth maried to John Appleyard. — Brigett maried to John Calabutt. |

| Thomas Hogan sonne & heyre. | Anne. |

# Conyers.

ARMS. *Azure, a maunch or, in chief a crescent of the second surmounted by another gules.*

CREST. *A sinister wing gules, differenced as the arms.*

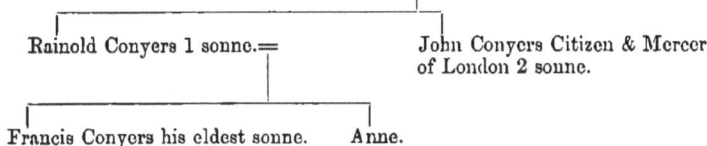

Francis Conyers descended of a younger howse=Anne da. of Blount sister to Sʳ
of Conyers of Horneby in Yorkshier. | Richard Blount Knight.

Rainold Conyers 1 sonne.=

John Conyers Citizen & Mercer
of London 2 sonne.

Francis Conyers his eldest sonne.　Anne.

# Smythe.

ARMS. *Gules, on a chevron or between three bezants three crosses pattée fitchée, in chief a martlet of the second.*

CREST. *A dexter arm couped at the elbow per pale or and gules, the cuff argent, holding in the hand proper a griffin's head erased azure, beaked and charged with a martlet or.*

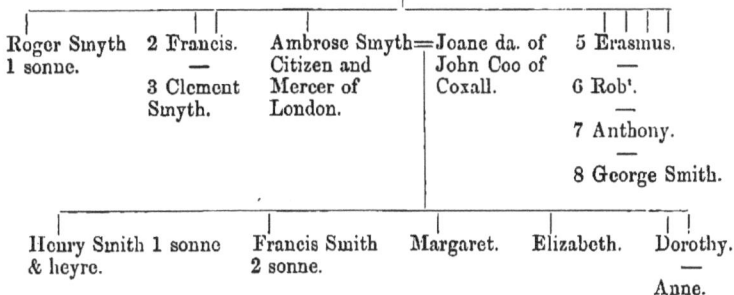

John Hares *alias* Smyth of Withcock=Dorothy da. of Richard Cave of
in com. Leic. gent. | Stanford Esq.

Roger Smyth　2 Francis.
1 sonne.　　　　—
　　　　　3 Clement
　　　　　Smyth.

Ambrose Smyth=Joane da. of
Citizen and　John Coo of
Mercer of　　Coxall.
London.

5 Erasmus.
—
6 Robᵗ.
—
7 Anthony.
—
8 George Smith.

Henry Smith 1 sonne
& heyre.

Francis Smith
2 sonne.

Margaret.　Elizabeth.　Dorothy.
　　　　　　　　　　　　—
　　　　　　　　　　　Anne.

# Candeler.

ARMS. *Argent, three pellets in bend cotised sable between two pellets impaling (for Lock). Quarterly:—1 and 4. Per fess azure and or, a pale counterchanged, in the first three falcons rising and holding in their mouths a padlock of the second. 2 and 3. Sable, a chevron between three conies' heads erased argent.* (SPENCER.)

CREST. *A goat's head couped sable, attired argent.*

Ric. Candeler.=— da. of — Lock.

# Holme.

ARMS. *Quarterly :—1 Barry of eight or and azure, on a canton argent, a chaplet gules. 2. Argent, a chevron azure within a bordure engrailed sable. 3. Gules, a cross engrailed argent, in the dexter chief a crescent or. 4. Or, three cocks gules, over all a mullet for difference.*
CREST. *A lion's head couped or, charged with a mullet for difference, ensigned with a cap of maintenance azure, turned up ermine.*

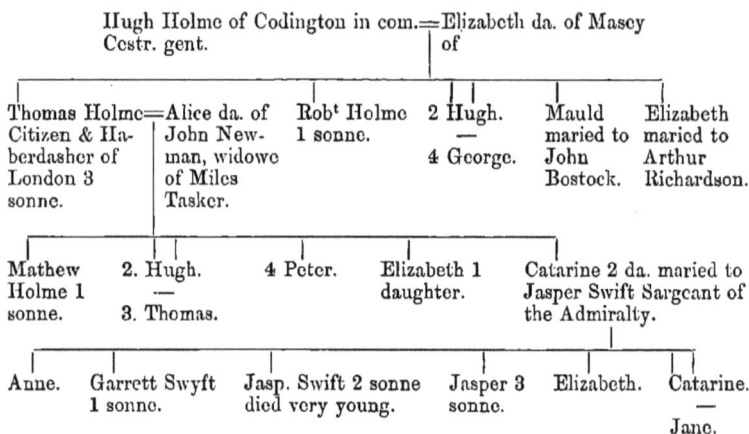

Hugh Holme of Codington in com.=Elizabeth da. of Masey
Cestr. gent. | of

Thomas Holme=Alice da. of | Robᵗ Holme | 2 Hugh. | Mauld | Elizabeth
Citizen & Ha- | John New- | 1 sonne. | — | maried to | maried to
berdasher of | man, widowe | | 4 George. | John | Arthur
London 3 | of Miles | | | Bostock. | Richardson.
sonne. | Tasker.

Mathew | 2. Hugh. | 4 Peter. | Elizabeth 1 | Catarine 2 da. maried to
Holme 1 | — | | daughter. | Jasper Swift Sargeant of
sonne. | 3. Thomas. | | | the Admiralty.

Anne. | Garrett Swyft | Jasp. Swift 2 sonne | Jasper 3 | Elizabeth. | Catarine.
| 1 sonne. | died very young. | sonne. | | —
| | | | | Jane.

# Saunders.

ARMS. *Per chevron sable and argent, three elephants' heads erased counterchanged, tusked or, a crescent for difference.*
CREST. *An elephant's head erased sable, ears and tusks argent, charged with a crescent for difference.*

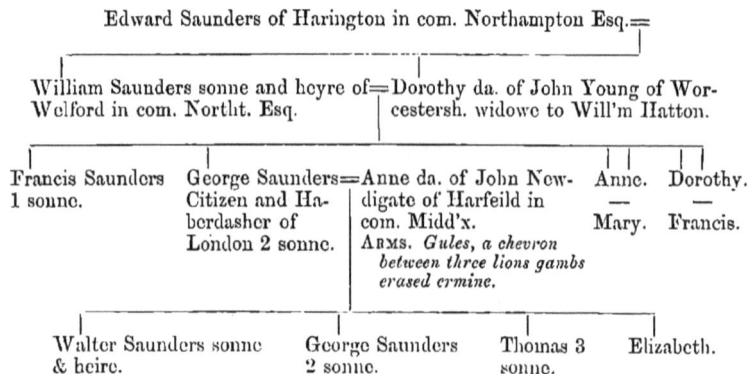

Edward Saunders of Harington in com. Northampton Esq.=

William Saunders sonne and heyre of=Dorothy da. of John Young of Wor-
Welford in com. Northt. Esq. | cestersh. widowe to Will'm Hatton.

Francis Saunders | George Saunders=Anne da. of John New- | Anne. | Dorothy.
1 sonne. | Citizen and Ha- | digate of Harfeild in | — | —
| berdasher of | com. Midd'x. | Mary. | Francis.
| London 2 sonne. | ARMS. *Gules, a chevron*
| | *between three lions gambs*
| | *erased ermine.*

Walter Saunders sonne | George Saunders | Thomas 3 | Elizabeth.
& heire. | 2 sonne. | sonne.

# Weaver.

ARMS. *Quarterly :*—1 *and* 4. *Or, on a fess azure between two cotices gules as many garbs of the field.* 2. *Azure, on a bend between two cotices argent three escallops gules.* (BOHUN.) 3. *Sable, a lion rampant, double queued argent,—over all a crescent for difference.* (WASTNEYS.)
CREST. *An antelope passant ermine, attired or, supporting with the dexter foot an escutcheon or.*

Walter Weaver of Herefordshire Esq.═

Walter Weaver sonne and═Joane da. and heyre of Gilbert Bohun of Shropshier
heyre of Walter. & of Margaret his wife da. & heyre of Tho. Wastneys
of Shropshier Esq.

Walter Weaver sonne &     Thomas Weaver 2 sonne.═Margaret da. of Richard
heyre.                                          Wisham Knight.

Walter Weaver.═Mauld da. of John Burghill Esq.

Thomas Weaver.═Anne da. of Delabere.

John Weaver.═Jane da. of James Apleby.

Jenkin Weaver 1═Margarett da. of Robt    Griff.   3. Walter.   Henry 4 sonne.
sonne.          Nanton.

John Weaver   Griffith Weaver 2 sonne of Pres-═Ellen da. of   Hugh     Ellen.
1 sonne.      tene in Herefordshier & Rad-       John Sadler.  3 sonne.
              nock.

John Weaver of London gent. sonne & heire═Alice da. of Thomas Anton, Clarke
of Griffith.                               of the Wards.

John Weaver sonne   Thomas 2 sonne.   George 3.   James 4.   Anne.   Catharine.
& heire.

## Hoðsðon.

ARMS. *Argent, a bend wavy gules between two horseshoes azure.*
CREST. *A man's head proper couped at the shoulders, vested azure, collared or, on the*
*head a cap of maintenance of the last turned up with fur proper.*

Thomas Hodsdon descended of Hodsdon of Hodsdon in Hertfordshier Esq.=

Simon Hodsdon his only sonne of Hodsdon and=Joane da. of John Etheredge of
of Edgeworth in com. Mid. ar.                     | Edgeworth.

| Nicholas | Elizab. da. of=Christopher=Alice da. of Alex. | Custance 1 da. ma- |
| Hodsden | Wᵐ Blunt of   Hodsdon   Carleill of London. | ried to Michael |
| 1 sonne | Osbaston in   Citizen and   ARMS. *Or, on a cross* | Moseley. |
| duxit | comit. Leic.   Haber-   *engrailed gules five* | — |
| filiam | vidua Saun-   dasher of   *martlets of the field,* | Anne maried to |
| Mayne | ders.   London 2   *in the first and* | Richard Webbe. |
| de com. | sonne.   *fourth quarters a* | — |
| Hertf. | *rose, in the second* | Grace maried to |
|  | *and third a griffin's* | Widow of Bucking- |
|  | *head erased of the* | hamshier. |
|  | *second.* | |

Vrsula sole daughter=Sʳ John Lee sonne of Tho. Leigh
and heyre.                | of Stonley in com. Warr.

Thomas Lee=Mary da. of Sʳ Thomas Egerton
son to my Lord Chancellor.

| 2 Henry Hoddesdon Rector Eccl'iæ | 3 Xpofer | John | Thomas | 5 Edward |
| de Iseldon al's Islington Anne da. | Hodsdon | Hodsdon. | Hoddes- | Hodsdon |
| of Robert Sibthorpe his wife.  She | Attorney | = | don 4 | Citizen & |
| was before twise maried first to | in the | Jane | sonne. | Draper of |
| Richard Martyn after to John | King's | Hay- | = | London. |
| Nicholas sonne & heire of Sir | Bench. | wood. | da. of | = |
| Ambrose Nicholas Mayor of Lon- | | | Markes | Anne da. of |
| don. | | | of Sur- | — Richard- |
| | | | rey. | son. |

3 Jane.   1 Brigett.   2 Eliz.   John Hodson.   2 Xpofer.

3 Thomas.   4 Edward.

# Hartford.

ARMS. *Barry nebulé of six or and azure, on a chief sable three stags' heads caboshed or.*

CREST. *A dexter arm erect couped at the elbow, vested per pale argent and gules, holding in the hand sable a stag's horn.*

Robert Hartford of Huntingdon gent.=

| | | | |
|---|---|---|---|
| Robert Hartford 2 sonne. | John Hartford Citizen and Mar-=Joane da. of Wood-chantaylor of London 1 sonne. | land of London. | William Hartford. |

William Hartford.    Elizabeth.

# Heath.

ARMS. *Per chevron sable and or, in chief two mullets pierced of the second, in base a heathcock of the first combed and wattled gules, a crescent of the last for difference.*

CREST. *A heathcock's head erased or, combed and wattled gules, a crescent sable for difference.*

John Heath of Twickenham in=Agnes da. of Lee & by her
Midlesex gent.      had issue.

| | | | | |
|---|---|---|---|---|
| John Heath 1 sonne. | Stephen Heath of=Agnes da. of — Myldemay of Chelmesford London, gent.  brother of Sir Walter Mildmay's father. | | | |

| | | | | |
|---|---|---|---|---|
| Thomas Heathe 1 sonne. | William Heathe 2 sonne. | Mary maried to Laurence Tynes of London Grocer. | Margaret. | Elizabeth. —  Agnes. |

# Partridge.

ARMS. *Gules, on a bend between two lions rampant or three parrots vert, beaked and legged gules.*

CREST. *Out of a rose gules stalked and leaved vert, a lion's head couped or.*

Anne da. of=Affabel Partridge of London Esq.=Margery da. of Gilbard of
Fildus 1      and Principall goldsmith vnto   Sussex.
wife.         our Sou'eyne Lady Quene      ARMS. *Argent a talbot passant*
              Elizabeth.                    *sable, on a chief indented of the*
                                            *second three besants.*

| | | |
|---|---|---|
| Thomas Partridge his sonne and heire. | Ellen maried to Thomas Bartellett of London. | Mary maried to Thomas Wadnall of London. |

# Tuck.

Arms. *Quarterly :—1 and 4. Argent, on a chevron between three greyhounds' heads erased sable, collared or, as many plates. 2. Per fess or and azure, a lion rampant billetté counterchanged. 3. Or, a cross engrailed gules.*

John Tuck of Kent had issue.=

John Tuck sonne and heire had issue=

Rafe Tuck 1 sonne and heire.

Thomas Tuck of=daughter and heyre of Goldwell and Kent 2 sonne. | of his wife da. and heyre of Hawte.

Rafe Tuck 1 sonne.

John Tuck of Kent Gent.=da. and coheyre of 3 sonne. | Walworth.

Richard Tuck 2 sonne.

John Tuck sonne and heire of John=Cecily da. to Sʳ Tho. Kempe of Wye.

Francis Tuck 1 sonne.

Nicholas Tuck, 2=Mary da. of sonne, Citizen | Bennet of and Skinner | Calleis. of London.

Richard Tuck 3 sonne.

Clare wife of Nicholas Moore.

Margaret married to Tho. Odyon of Kent.

John Tuck eldest sonne. 2 Nicholas. 3 Thomas. Mary. Clare.

# Hoskyns.

Arms. *Per pale gules and azure, a chevron engrailed or, between three lions rampant argent.*

Crest. *A cock's head or pelletté, combed and wattled gules, between two wings expanded of the first.*

Thomas Hoskyns of Monmouth=Jane da. of Catchmade of in Wales. | Gloucestershire.

Charles Hos-= — daughter of kyns 1 | Inglosse. sonne.

George Hoskyns 2 sonne.

Joane maried first to John ap Owen 2 to William Jenkyns 3 to John Knithlyn.

Inglosse Coate his sonnes wife.
*Barry of six or and azure, on a canton argent five billets in saltire of the first.*

# Gilbert.

ARMS. *Azure, a chevron ermine, between three eagles displayed or.*
CREST. *An eagle displayed azure.*

Richard Gilbert of Somerson in com. Suff. gent.=Anne da. of .... Cortnoll.

| Henry Gilbert 1 sonne. | Henry Gilbert 3 sonne Citizen and Goldsmith of London. | =Elizabeth da. of . . . Howes. ARMS. *Argent, a chevron between three wolves' heads couped sable.* | Edward Gilbert 2 sonne. | =Alice da. of Bond of Warwicksh. |

| Sir John Gilbert of Suff. | Dorothy 1 da. mar. to S<sup>r</sup> George Speak of Som'stshire. | .... filius objit juvenis. | Elizabeth 1 marr. to .... Colby and after to S<sup>r</sup> Michael Mollyns of Wallingford in com. Bark. |

---

# Mabbe.

ARMS. *Per pale gules and azure, a tiger passant argent.*
CREST. *A wivern with wings endorsed or pellettée.*

John Mabbe of Clayton in comitatu=Joane da. of . . . Goble of
Sussex. Sussex.

| John Mabbe 1 sonne Citizen and goldsmith of London. | =Isabell da. of Richard Colley of Shropshier. | Richard. 2 sonne. | Nicholas. 3 sonne. |

| John Mabbe of London gent., 1 sonne. | =Martha da. of William Denham of London. | Richard 2 sonne. | 3. Stephen. — 4. Rob<sup>t</sup> — 5. Edward. — 6. Will<sup>m</sup>. | Mary mar. to John Dolman. | Susan. | Catarine. |

John Mabbe 1 sonne. 2. William.

---

# Castelyn.

ARMS. *Quarterly :—*1 and 4. *Sable, on a chevron or between three castles therefrom issuing as many demi-lions argent, three anchors azure.* 2 and 3. *Or, on a mount vert an eagle displayed sable.*

Castelyn of London gent.=

## Heton.

ARMS. *Argent, six trefoils slipped vert.*

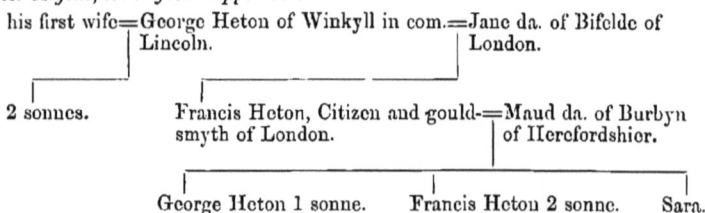

```
his first wife=George Heton of Winkyll in com.=Jane da. of Bifelde of
              |    Lincoln.                           |    London.
    _____|_____            _____|_____
   |                   |         |
2 sonnes.         Francis Heton, Citizen and gould-=Maud da. of Burbyn
                  smyth of London.                  |  of Herefordshior.
               _____|_____
              |                        |                     |
        George Heton 1 sonne.    Francis Heton 2 sonne.    Sara.
```

## Wasse.

ARMS. *Quarterly :—1 and 4. Barry of six argent and gules. 2. Argent, on a saltire
gules between four eagles displayed azure a mullet for difference.* (HAMPDEN.)
*3. Argent, on a saltire gules between four door-staples sable an escallop of the
field.* (STOUGHTON.)
CREST *A demi-lion rampant argent, ducally gorged azure.*

```
Christopher Wasse of Wickham=Catarine da. and heyre of Thomas Hampden
in com. Buck. gent. father of | sonne and heyre of Thomas Hampden and of
John Wasse.                   | Margaret his wife sister and heyre of Wᵐ
                              | Stocton al's Stockton sive Stoughton.
           _____|
          |
    John Wasse of Wickham gent.=Margaret da. of Holte of Hampshire.
                               |
   _____|_____
  |                             |                        |
John Wasse of Wickham gent. sonne=Clare da. of . . .   Elizabeth maried to
and heire.                      | Welles.              . . . Harison.
         _____|
        |
   Christofer Wasse, citizen and goldsmith of London.
```

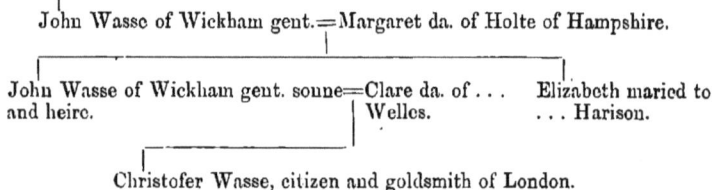

## Jackson.

ARMS. *Gules, a fess argent between three jackdaws proper.*

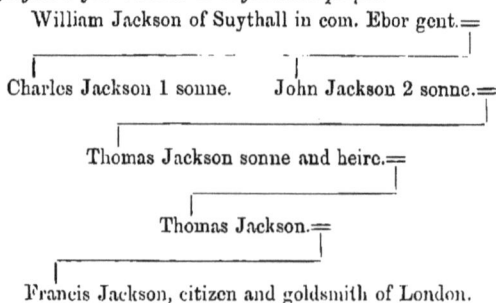

```
        William Jackson of Suythall in com. Ebor gent.=
                                                       |
   _____       |
  |                             |                 |
Charles Jackson 1 sonne.   John Jackson 2 sonne.=
                                                 |
         _____|
        |
   Thomas Jackson sonne and heire.=
                                   |
         _____|
        |
   Thomas Jackson.=
                   |
   _____|
  |
Francis Jackson, citizen and goldsmith of London.
```

# Gaynsford.

ARMS. *Argent, on a chevron gules between three greyhounds sable, a crescent for difference or.*

CREST. *A demi-maiden couped below the waist, habited gules, crined or, holding in her dexter hand a wreath vert, and in her sinister a rose-branch proper.*

Henry Gaynsford of Cassolton in com.=Catarine da. of — Wilford of London.
Surr. gent.

| Catarine. | Robert Gayns- ford 1 sonne. | Henry Gayns-=Mary ford 2 soune, da. of Citizen and John- Goldsmith of son of London. Lon- don. | | Nicholas 3 sonne. — Francis 4. | Elizabeth maried to Richard Thomas. — Alice maried to John Cotingham. — Anne maried to Tho^s Cotingham. |

Thomas Gaynsford sonne and heire.

---

# Muschamp.

ARMS. *Quarterly :—1 and 4. Or, three bars gules, on the first bar a martlet of the field for difference. 2 and 3. Argent, on a chevron gules between three lozenges sable, as many martlets or.*

CREST. *A mountain cat proper, tied round the neck with a scarf argent, charged on the breast with a martlet for difference.*

da. of Harman his==William Muschamp of Camberwell in com Surr.=wydowe of
3 wife.            maried to his 1 wife the da. of Scott but had     Nynnes 2
                   no issue by her.                                  wife.

| Edward Mus- champ 1 sonne. | Thomas Muschamp=Catarine Citizen and Gold- da. of smith of London. Louday. | Xpofer Mus- champ 3 sonne. | Rafe Mus- champ. | John Mus- champ. |

Jane 1 da. maried to Tho.       Susan 2 da. maried to Henry Toppesfeild
Crymes of London.               Citizen and Marchant of London.

---

G

# Metcalfe.

ARMS. *Argent, on a fess vert between three calves sable, a leopard's face between two annulets or.*

CREST. *A demi-sea-calf sable, purfled or.*

Thomas Metcalfe gent. Citizen and=Alice da. of Tho. Cook of Tanton.
Goldsmith of London.

    ARMS. *Azure, on a chevron engrailed argent between two cotises or, and three cinquefoils pierced ermine, two lions combattant purpure.*

Anne maried, wife of Richard Elkyn of London, Skynner.=

| Thomas Elkyn. | Alice. | Richard Elkyn. | John Elkyn. |
|---|---|---|---|

# Gardenor.

ARMS. *Quarterly:—Gules and azure, in the second and third quarters a griffin segreant or, holding in the dexter claw a ring gemmed of the last, over all, on a bend cotised of the last, a leopard's face, holding in the mouth a round buckle between two fleurs-de-lis gules.*

CREST. *A leopard passant argent pelletté, holding in the dexter paw a pineapple or, stalked and leaved vert.*

Thomas Gardenor Citizen and Gouldsmith of London maried to=Elizabeth da. of
his 2 wife Beatrix da. of Mayo of London.           Tarte.

Thomas Gardenor of Saffron=da. of Nicholas Whitney    Richard Gardner
Walden in Essex 1 sonne.   of London.        2 sonne.

# Anthony.

ARMS. *Argent, a leopard's head gules between two flaunches sable.*
CREST. *A demi-goat proper, charged with a bezant armed and attired or.*
(ON A SMALL SHIELD.) *" They bore this first."*   *Argent, a leopard's head gules between two flaunches sable, on the dexter a rose, on the sinister a mullet or, a crescent in chief for difference.*

William Anthony borne at Colen in Germany.⊤

| Margarett da. and=coheyre of Edward Ridge of Staffordshier. | Derick Anthony was borne at St Kathe-rines by ye Tower cheif graver of the Mynt and scales to King Edward VI., Q. Mary and Q. Elizabeth. | Elizabeth da. & heir of Richard Erleyal's Ellerick of Lincolnshire. |

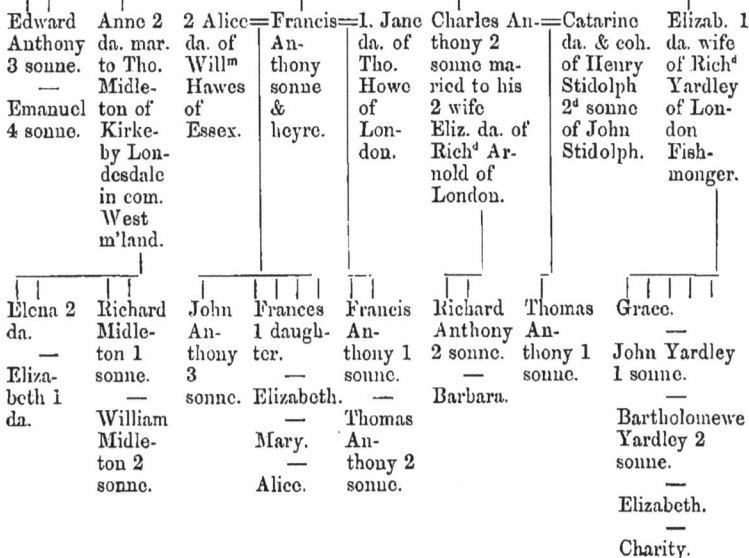

| Edward Anthony 3 sonne. — Emanuel 4 sonne. | Anne 2 da. mar. to Tho. Midle-ton of Kirke-by Lon-desdale in com. West m'land. | 2 Alice=da. of Willm Hawes of Essex. | Francis=An-thony sonne & heyre. | 1. Jane da. of Tho. Howe of Lon-don. | Charles An-=thony 2 sonne ma-ried to his 2 wife Eliz. da. of Richd Ar-nold of London. | Catarine da. & coh. of Henry Stidolph 2d sonne of John Stidolph. | Elizab. 1 da. wife of Richd Yardley of Lon-don Fish-monger. |

| Elena 2 da. — Eliza-beth 1 da. | Richard Midle-ton 1 sonne. — William Midle-ton 2 sonne. | John An-thony 3 sonne. | Frances 1 daugh-ter. — Elizabeth. — Mary. — Alice. | Francis An-thony 1 sonne. — Thomas An-thony 2 sonne. | Richard Anthony 2 sonne. — Barbara. | Thomas An-thony 1 sonne. | Grace. — John Yardley 1 sonne. Bartholomewe Yardley 2 sonne. — Elizabeth. — Charity. |

---

# (Edwardes.)

ARMS. *Argent, a fess ermines between three martlets sable.*
CREST. *A lion's gamb, couped and erect ermine, grasping a goat's leg erased sable, armed or.*

Beneath this coat is written in pencil :—

" It is Edwardes Coate."

---

# Dalton.

ARMS. *Azure semé of crosses crosslet, a lion rampant reguardant argent, charged on the breast with a mullet gules.*
CREST. *A dragon's head vert between two wings or, pelletté.*

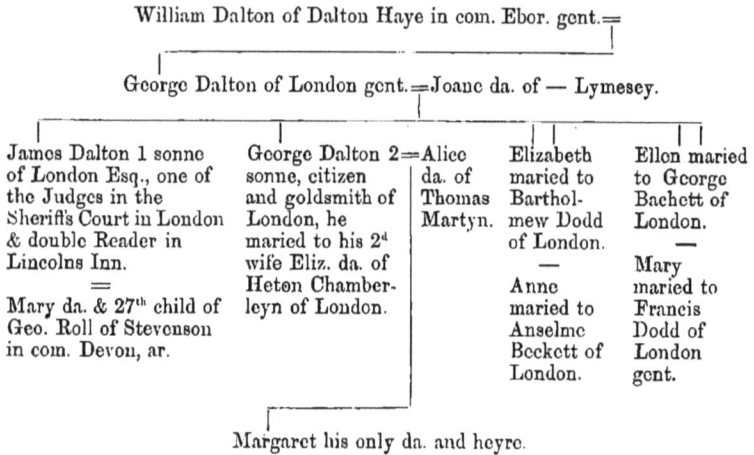

William Dalton of Dalton Haye in com. Ebor. gent.=

George Dalton of London gent.=Joane da. of — Lymesey.

| James Dalton 1 sonne of London Esq., one of the Judges in the Sheriff's Court in London & double Reader in Lincolns Inn. | George Dalton 2=Alice sonne, citizen and goldsmith of London, he maried to his 2ᵈ wife Eliz. da. of Heton Chamberleyn of London. | Elizabeth da. of Thomas Martyn. | Ellen maried to George Bachett of London. |
| --- | --- | --- | --- |
| = Mary da. & 27ᵗʰ child of Geo. Roll of Stevenson in com. Devon, ar. | | maried to Bartholmew Dodd of London. — Anne maried to Anselme Beckett of London. | — Mary maried to Francis Dodd of London gent. |

Margaret his only da. and heyre.

---

# Smyth.

ARMS. *Argent, a cross compony counter compony or and azure, between four lions passant sable.*
CREST. *Out of a ducal coronet or a swan close ermine, beaked gules.*

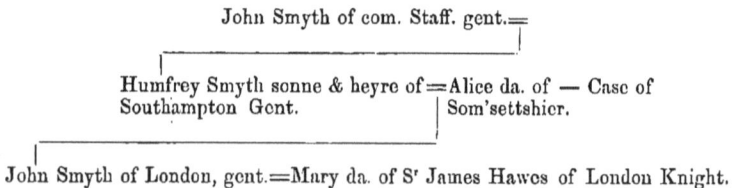

John Smyth of com. Staff. gent.=

Humfrey Smyth sonne & heyre of=Alice da. of — Case of
Southampton Gent.       Som'settshier.

John Smyth of London, gent.=Mary da. of Sʳ James Hawes of London Knight.

---

# Carrowe.

ARMS. *Or, three lioncels passant in pale sable, a bordure compony of the same.*
CREST. *A mainmast broken, the round top set off with palisadoes or, headed argent, a lion issuant thereout sable, collared per pale of the first and second.*

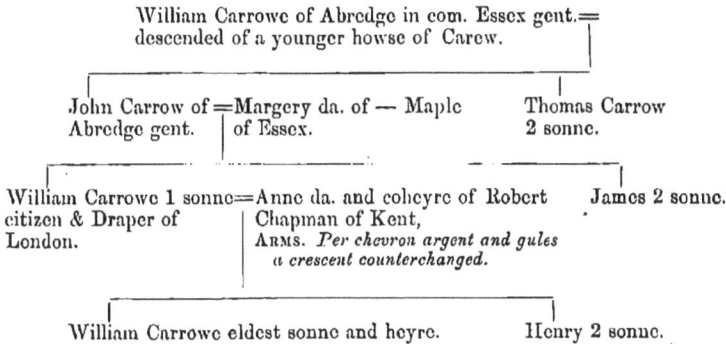

William Carrowe of Abredge in com. Essex gent.=
descended of a younger howse of Carew.

John Carrow of =Margery da. of — Maple    Thomas Carrow
Abredge gent.   of Essex.                2 sonne.

William Carrowe 1 sonne=Anne da. and cohcyre of Robert    James 2 sonne.
citizen & Draper of      Chapman of Kent,
London.            ARMS. *Per chevron argent and gules
                 a crescent counterchanged.*

William Carrowe eldest sonne and heyre.    Henry 2 sonne.

# Pope.

ARMS. *Quarterly 1 and 4. Argent, three popinjays vert, winged or, within a bordure engrailed azure bezanté. 2 and 3. Or, three buckles sable.*
CREST. *A harlequin habited argent and gules, paleways counterchanged, holding in his dexter arm a scimitar of the first, hilted or.*

Francis Pope of London gent. and Draper=Grace da. of Robert Deane
to Queen Elizabeth maried to his 1 wife    of London grocer and
Agnes da. of John Dowse and by her    hath no issue.
had no issue.

# Mansbridge.

ARMS. *Quarterly argent and vert, four eagles displayed counterchanged.*

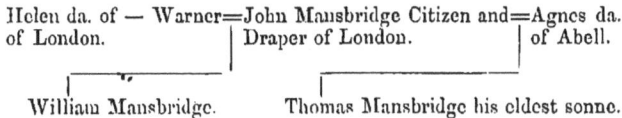

Helen da. of — Warner=John Mansbridge Citizen and=Agnes da.
of London.         Draper of London.      of Abell.

William Mansbridge.    Thomas Mansbridge his eldest sonne.

## Luddington.

ARMS. *Quarterly :—1 and 4. Paly of six argent and gules, on a chief of the second a lion passant guardant of the first. 2. Argent, two bars gules, on a canton of the second a cross patonce or.* (KIRKEBY.) *3. Per fess azure and or, a pale counterchanged, on the first three lions rampant of the second* (WHETTILL), *"impaled with Rowe of London."*

| Henry Ludyngton gent. first= | Joane da. and heyre of William Kirkeby of |
|---|---|
| husband to this Joane, and | Kirkeby in Yorkshier which William Kirkeby |
| by her had issue. | maried Alice da. & heyre of Whettill. This Joane |
| | was after maried to S$^r$ William Laxton, Knight. |

| Nicholas Luddington=Avis his | Joane first maried to — | Anne maried to |
|---|---|---|
| his sonne and heyre    wife. | Machell, Sheriff of London, | S$^r$ Thomas |
| Citizen of London. | after to S$^r$ Thomas | Lodge Knight. |
| | Chamberleyne, Knight. | |

## Horspoole.

ARMS. *Sable, on a chevron argent three lions' heads erased of the field.*
CREST. *A demi-pegasus erased, wings expanded ermine, girded round the loins with a ducal coronet or.*

John Horspoole of London, gent.=Hawis da. of — Baker.

Symon Horspoole citizen and=Elizabeth da. of John Smyth of
Draper of London.    Cossam in com. Wiltesh.

| William Horspoole 1 sonne. | 2 Simon. | 3 Thomas. | Elizabeth. | Mary. | Hawis. |
|---|---|---|---|---|---|

## Hodgeson.

ARMS. *Gules, three scimitars in pale argent, hilted gules, the points of the first and third and the hilt of the second to the dexter side, within a bordure engrailed argent pelletté.*
CREST. *A dexter arm erect, couped at the elbow, habited bendy sinister of four argent and gules, holding in the hand proper a covered cup or.*

Thomas Hodgeson of Yorkeshier gent.=Agnes da. of Robert Cooke of Essex.

William Hodgson, citizen and Merchant=Elizabeth da. of Fowke Wall
taylor of London.    of Cradeley in Shropshire.

# Parker.

ARMS. *Argent, a chevron gules between three mullets sable, on a chief azure three stags' heads caboshed of the field.*
CREST. *A reindeer's head erased per fess argent and gules, attired or.*

John Parker of Dantrey in com Northampton=Margery da. of Vincent Crosse gent. descended of Parker of Norton in | of Warwickshier.
com. Ebor.

William Parker his sonne and heyre.=Margery da. of William Allen of London.

# Pullison.

[ARMS. *Per pale argent and sable, three lions rampant counterchanged.*
CREST. *Out of a ducal coronet gules a demi-peacock, wings expanded or.*]

S<sup>r</sup> Thomas Pullison Knight Sheriff and after Mayor of London.=

# Brett.

ARMS. *Argent semé of crosses crosslet fitché, a lion rampant gules.*

Alexander Brett of Whitstanton in com. Deuon= — da. of Rosemaderos.

John Brett 1 sonne.　Robert Brett of=Elizabeth da. of Edward Bush of　Symon Brett
Lincolnshier gent.　Sison 3 brother to the Bushes of　2 sonne.
Hohum.

Robert Brett 1 sonne=Elizabeth da. of Reginald Highgate　Margaret wife of
Citizen & Mar-　of Essex.　— Veale of Lanca-
chantaylor of　ARMS. *Gules, two bars argent, over all*　shier.
London.　*on a bend or a torteau between two*
*leopards' heads azure.*

John Brett his eldest sonne.　2 William.　3 Robert.　4 Richard.　Elizabeth.　Catharine.

# Albaney.

ARMS. *Ermine, on a fess between three cinquefoils gules, a greyhound courant or.*
CREST. *Out of a ducal coronet gules, a dolphin embowed argent, purfled or.*

William Albaney of London gent. & Marchantaylor, he=Thomas da. of Richard
maried to his 2 wife Joane da. of Robert Cordall of | Buttle of London.
London.

| Francis Albany 1 sonne. | William Albany 2 sonne. | Robert 3 sonne. | 1. Mary. | 2. Judith. |

---

# Bragden.

ARMS. *Argent, a lion passant azure between three fleurs-de-lis gules.*
CREST. *A boar issuant out of a rock proper.*

John Bragden of London gent.=Margery da. of Thomas Body of Worcester.
ARMS. *Argent, on a fess azure three pelicans vulning themselves or.*

| Thomas Brogden 1 sonne & heyre. | 2 Edward. | 3 Richard. | 4 William. | Avis maried to Nicholas Tetlowe of London. | Mary. |

---

# Farrington.

ARMS. *Quarterly :—1 and 4. Argent, a chevron gules between three leopards' heads
purpure. 2 and 3. Gules, three cinquefoils argent.*
CREST. *A wivern sans wings, tail extended vert.*

John Farrington of Sussex descended of a younger howse=Margaret his wife.
of Farrington in com. Lanc.

| John Farrington Citizen & Clothworker of London. | =Alice da. of Sr Alexander Avenon of London Knight. | George a preist 2 sonne. | Richard Farrington 3 sonne Alderman of London 1609. | Sibill. wife of — Covert. | Mary maried to . William Danser. |

| Alexander Farrington 1 sonne. | 2 John. | 3 Thomas. | Elizabeth. | Mirabell. | Marye mar. to — Martindale. |

# Lucar.

ARMS. *Quarterly :—1 and 4. Argent, a chevron sable between three nags' heads erased gules, bridled or. 2 and 3. Argent, a fess nebulé azure, in chief a lion's head erased of the last between two mascles and one in base gules.*
CREST. *A dexter arm couped at the elbow, vested per pale azure and gules, holding in the hand propor a lure argent, stringed of the second, ringed and knotted or.*

Joane da. of Thomas=Emanuel Lucar=Elizabeth da. of Paule Withipole and by
Turnbull. | of London Esqʳ. | her had issue.
ARMS. *Or, a fess* | | ARMS. *Quarterly :—1 and 4. Per pale or*
*between three bulls* | | *and gules, three lions passant in pale with-*
*winged azure.* | | *in a bordure counterchanged. 2. Azure,*
| | *three bars or, over all on a bend engrailed*
| | *gules three pheons argent. 3. Azure, a*
| | *cross moline between four crosses patté or.*

| Ciprian Lucar. | 4 Mark. — 5 John. | Martha. — Mary. | Emanuel Lucar, his eldest sonne. | Henry 2 sonne. | Mary wife of Richᵈ Pigram. — Jane maried to William Rowe of London. | Filia. |

# Prowze.

ARMS. *Quarterly of six :—1 and 6. Argent, three lions rampant sable. 2. Argent, a bend gules, on a chief vert two cinquefoils or. 3. Azure, a bend per bend indented gules and argent between six escallops or.* (CREWYS.) *4. Argent, a fess dancetté in chief two martlets sable. 5. Azure, a chevron argent between three pears or.* (CALMADY.)

Christopher Prowze of Chagford in Cornwall.=

John Prowez of Rie.=Alice da. of — Baseden of Rie.

| John Prowse 1 sonne. | Thomas Prowez Citizen and=Alice da. of John Smyth of Vintener of London. | Tringe in com. Buck. |

| Elizabeth. | Mercy. | Catarine. | Judith. | Xpofer. |

# Hilles.

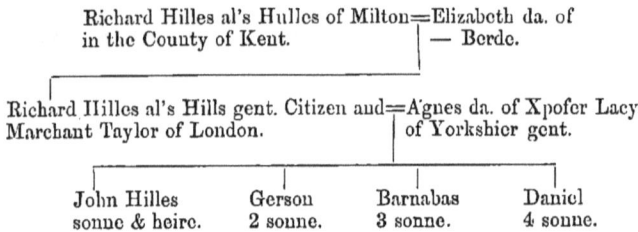

Richard Hilles al's Hulles of Milton=Elizabeth da. of
in the County of Kent. | — Berde.

Richard Hilles al's Hills gent. Citizen and=Agnes da. of Xpofer Lacy
Marchant Taylor of London. | of Yorkshier gent.

| John Hilles | Gerson | Barnabas | Daniel |
| sonne & heire. | 2 sonne. | 3 sonne. | 4 sonne. |

# Hall.

ARMS. *Argent semé of crosses crosslet, three talbots' heads erased sable.*

Thomas Hall of Warnam in the County of Sussex.=Margaret da. of Pawthorne.

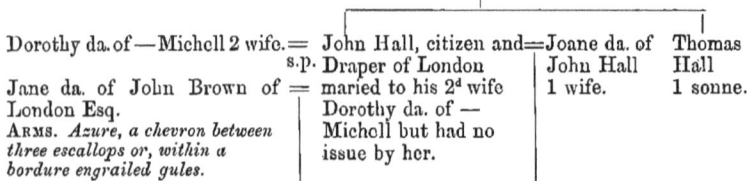

Dorothy da. of — Michell 2 wife. =   John Hall, citizen and=Joane da. of   Thomas
                          s.p.  Draper of London | John Hall   Hall
Jane da. of John Brown of  =  maried to his 2ᵈ wife | 1 wife.   1 sonne.
London Esq.                   Dorothy da. of —
ARMS. *Azure, a chevron between*    Michell but had no
*three escallops or, within a*      issue by her.
*bordure engrailed gules.*

| John Hall 1 sonne. | 2 Humfry. | 3 Thomas, | Jane oldest daughter. |

# Hall.

ARMS. *Argent, a fess between two greyhounds courant sable.*
CREST. *Out of a ducal coronet or, a demi-greyhound sable collared of the first.*

John Hall of Skipton in Craven in Yorkshier.=Alice da. of Merslinge of Kent.

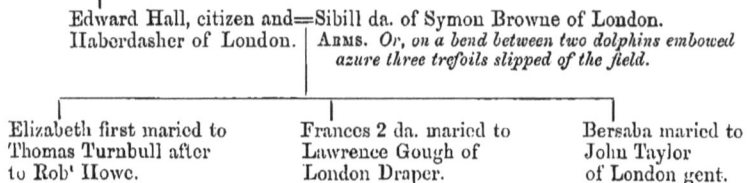

Edward Hall, citizen and=Sibill da. of Symon Browne of London.
Haberdasher of London. | ARMS. *Or, on a bend between two dolphins embowed*
                         *azure three trefoils slipped of the field.*

| Elizabeth first maried to | Frances 2 da. maried to | Bersaba maried to |
| Thomas Turnbull after | Lawrence Gough of | John Taylor |
| to Robᵗ Howe. | London Draper. | of London gent. |

## Rivell.

ARMS. *Per pale indented argent and sable, a chevron gules.*

Robert Rivell of Kellingesbery in com.=Catarine da. of John Russell of
Northt. | London.

Nicholas Rivell Citizen and grocer of London.=Audrey da. of John Michenar.

Robert Rivell sonne & heyre. | Emme.

## Jenkynson.

ARMS. *Azure, a fess wavy argent, in chief three estoiles or.*
CREST. *A seahorse assurgent per pale or and azure, crined gules.*

Anthony Jenkynson Citizen and Mercer=Judith da. of John Marshe of
of London. | London Esq.

Alice 1 da. | Mary 2 da.

## Marbury.

ARMS. *Quarterly of 9 :*—1. *Sable, a cross engrailed between four pheons argent.*
(MARBURY.) 2. *Or, on a fess engrailed azure three garbs of the field.* (MER-
BURY.) 3. *Barry nebulé of six or and sable.* (BLOUNT.) 4. *(Argent), two
wolves passant in pale (sable), on a bordure (gules) eight saltires couped (or).*
(AYALA.) 5. *Or, a four-towered castle azure.* (CASTILE.) 6. *Vair.* (BEAU-
CHAMP.) 7. *Argent, three fleurs-de-lis azure.* 8. *Argent, a fess and in chief
three covered cups gules.* 9. *Vert, a saltire engrailed argent.* (HAWLEY.)

William Merbury father of=Agnes da. & coheyre of Thomas Blount younger
Robert and Thomas | brother to Sᵣ William Blount, and of his wife
Marbury. | the da. & heyre of John Hawley.

Thomas Marbury Citizen &=Agnes da. of — Lynne   Robert Marbury 1
haberdasher of London. | of Northampton.    sonne.

| Christian married to Francis Withers. — Joh'nes Marbery. | Humfrey Mar-bury 2 sonne Citizen & haberdasher of London. | Anne da. of Alder-man Bankes of London. ARMS. *Sable, on a cross or between four fleurs-de-lis argent five ogresses.* | Anne 1ˢᵗ maried to — Bradley after to Armiger Wade. — Thomasin maried to Thomas Jennyns. | Alice wife of Tho. Mar-bury. — Elizabeth maried to Richards Ellis. |

## Jenkenson.

James Jenkensonne of Tourley in the⹀Elen daughter of — Danell of Kedsnape
County of Lankersheyer.     |     in the County of Lancas<sup>r</sup>.

Robartt Jenkenson of Tourley.⹀Brigett Whinyard of London.

S<sup>r</sup> Roburtt Jenkenson⹀Ann Mary Lee daughter of S<sup>r</sup> Rob. Lee of Billesley in
of Walcott in the     Worwickshyer 2 sonne of S<sup>r</sup> Rob<sup>t</sup> Lee, Maior of London
County of Oxford.     by Anne daughter of S<sup>r</sup> Th. Loe of Lond. Knight.

## Coleclogh.

ARMS. *Quarterly :—1 and 4. Argent, five eagles displayed in cross sable.   2 and 3.
Sable, a fess between three martlets argent* (LOCKWOOD); *over all a crescent
for difference.*
CREST. *A demi-eagle displayed sable, charged on the breast with a crescent or.*

John Coleclogh of Ingleton in the County⹀Anne da. and heyre of —
of Stafford.     |     Lockwood.

Richard Coleclogh of Ingleton and of⹀Aleonor da. of Sir John     Thomas Cole-
Blurton in com. Stafford.     |     Draycott Knight.     clogh.

| S<sup>r</sup> Anthony⹀ Coleclogh of Yngeton K<sup>t</sup>. | Richard 3 sonne. | 1 Catarine daughter & heyre of Edward Dalton of Calays 1 wife. | ⹀Mathew Coleclogh of London, draper maried to his 3<sup>rd</sup> wife Margaret or Mary da. of Warner of London & widow to Johnson. | 2. Margarett da. of Richard Bennett of Callais 2 wife. |
|---|---|---|---|---|
| S<sup>r</sup> Thomas Colecloghe, Knt. | John Cole-cloghe. | Catherine. | Richard Coleclough 6 sonne.<br>—<br>Richard 7 sonne.<br>—<br>Mary. | Anthony Colclogh alij Adam 2 sonne.  Tobias. | George.<br>—<br>Mathew. |

# Allen.

ARMS. *Quarterly :—1 and 4. Per fess gules and sable, a chevron rompu ermine between three griffins' heads erased argent. 2 and 3. Sable, a chevron ermine between three unicorns' heads erased argent.* (HEDD.)

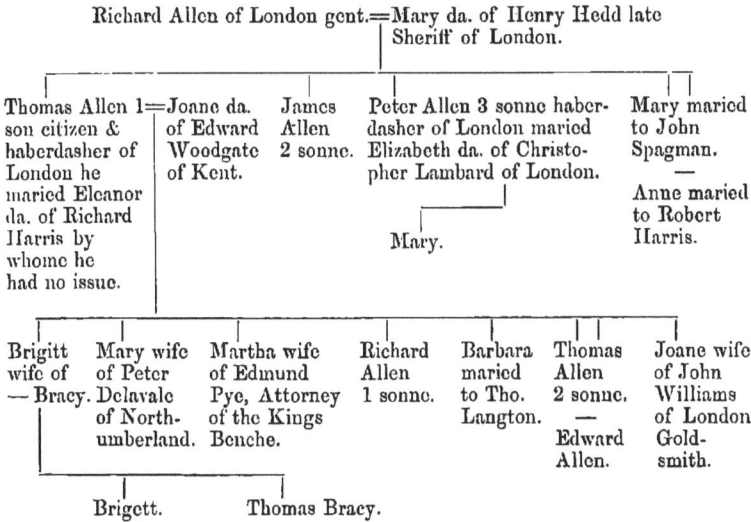

Richard Allen of London gent.=Mary da. of Henry Hedd late Sheriff of London.

Thomas Allen 1=Joane da. of Edward Woodgate of Kent.
son citizen & haberdasher of London he maried Eleanor da. of Richard Harris by whome he had no issue.

James Allen 2 sonne.

Peter Allen 3 sonne haberdasher of London maried Elizabeth da. of Christopher Lambard of London.
|
Mary.

Mary maried to John Spagman.
—
Anne maried to Robert Harris.

Brigitt wife of — Bracy.
|
Brigett.

Mary wife of Peter Delavale of Northumberland.

Martha wife of Edmund Pye, Attorney of the Kings Benche.
|
Thomas Bracy.

Richard Allen 1 sonne.

Barbara maried to Tho. Langton.

Thomas Allen 2 sonne.
—
Edward Allen.

Joane wife of John Williams of London Goldsmith.

# Witton.

ARMS. *Quarterly :—1 and 4. Sable, a water-bouget argent, in chief three bezants. 2 and 3. Argent, a fess gules between three bulls' heads couped sable.* CREST. *An owl argent, legged sable, ducally gorged or.*

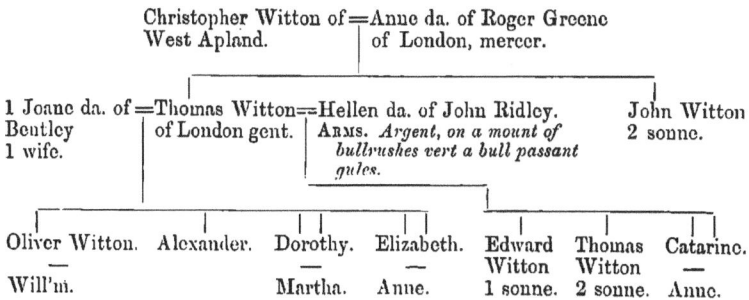

Christopher Witton of West Apland.=Anne da. of Roger Greene of London, mercer.

1 Joane da. of Beutley 1 wife.=Thomas Witton==Hellen da. of John Ridley. of London gent. ARMS. *Argent, on a mount of bullrushes vert a bull passant gules.*

John Witton 2 sonne.

Oliver Witton.
—
Will'm.

Alexander.
—

Dorothy.
—
Martha.

Elizabeth.
—
Anne.

Edward Witton 1 sonne.

Thomas Witton 2 sonne.

Catarine.
—
Anne.

# Harding.

ARMS. *Gules, three greyhounds courant in pale or, collared azure.*
CREST. *A demi-leopard rampant ermine, gorged with a collar azure bezanté, chain compony, counter-compony of the last.*

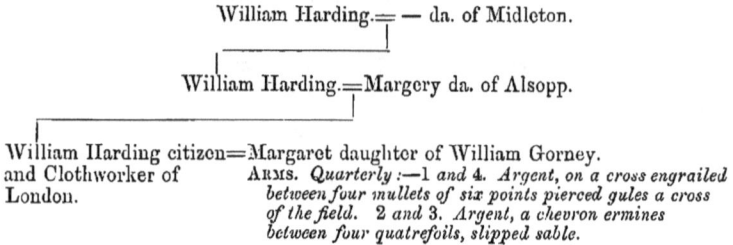

William Harding.═ — da. of Midleton.

William Harding.═Margery da. of Alsopp.

William Harding citizen═Margaret daughter of William Gorney.
and Clothworker of     ARMS. *Quarterly :—1 and 4. Argent, on a cross engrailed*
London.             *between four mullets of six points pierced gules a cross*
                *of the field. 2 and 3. Argent, a chevron ermines*
                *between four quatrefoils, slipped sable.*

# Redman.

ARMS. *Gules, three cushions ermine, tasselled or, in chief a fleur-de-lis of the last for difference.*

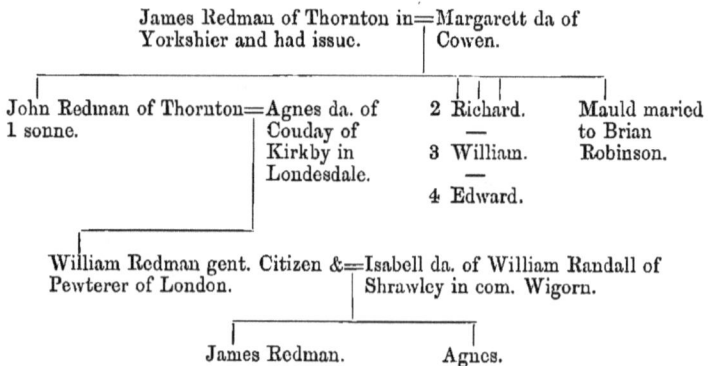

James Redman of Thornton in═Margarett da of
Yorkshier and had issue.    Cowen.

John Redman of Thornton═Agnes da. of    2 Richard.    Mauld maried
1 sonne.            Couday of       —        to Brian
              Kirkby in    3 William.    Robinson.
              Londesdale.      —
                          4 Edward.

William Redman gent. Citizen &═Isabell da. of William Randall of
Pewterer of London.        Shrawley in com. Wigorn.

James Redman.        Agnes.

# Dale.

ARMS. *Sable, on a chevron or between three cranes rising argent seven torteaux.*

Will'mus Dale de Bristowe.=. . . filia Winter.

Mathew Dale of =Mary da. of Chapman of Bathe
Bristowe gent. | in com. Som'set.

| Henry Dale son & heyre. = Emery da. of Cordall. | Elizab. maried to Gregory Isham of London, now of Branston in com. Northt. | John Dale= 2 sonne Citizen and haberdasher of London. | Elizabeth daughter of William Lane of London grocer. | Mathew 3= sonne Judge in Guildhall London A° 1612. | Margaret da. of William Cock of London. ARMS. *Quarterly gules and argent, in chief a a crescent for difference.* |

1 Elizabeth.    2 Alice.    3 Anne.       Matheus Dale.    Elizabeth maried to    Mary.
                                                            — Packer of London.

# Erdeswick.

ARMS. *Quarterly of six :—1. Argent, on a chevron gules five bezants. 2. Argent, a chevron between three eagles' heads erased sable. 3. Or, a chevron gules. 4. Gules, a fess between six crosses crosslet within a bordure or. 5. Or, two bends compony argent and gules. 6. Gules, a chevron wavy between three stags' heads caboshed argent.*
CREST. *Out of a ducal coronet gules a boar's head per pale argent and sable.*

Hugh Erdeswick father of =Joan da. of — Bassett
Hugh and John. | of Blore.

John Erdeswick 2 sonne.=       Hugh 1 sonne.

Richard Erdeswick.=Margaret da. of — Galamore.

Richard Erdeswick.=Joane da. of Edward    Helen mar. to
                   Bright of London.      William Rutter.

## Bramstone.

ARMS. *Or, on a fess sable three plates.*

CREST. *A tun fessways or, thereon a raven sable holding in his beak a carnation-branch proper.*

Hugh Bramstone of London, gent.═Elizabeth da. of — Norris of London.

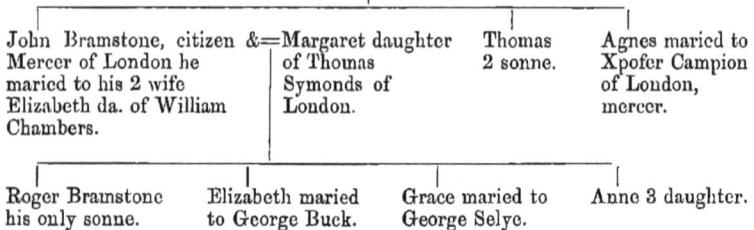

| | | | |
|---|---|---|---|
| John Bramstone, citizen Mercer of London he maried to his 2 wife Elizabeth da. of William Chambers. | &═Margaret daughter of Thomas Symonds of London. | Thomas 2 sonne. | Agnes maried to Xpofer Campion of London, mercer. |

| | | | |
|---|---|---|---|
| Roger Bramstone his only sonne. | Elizabeth maried to George Buck. | Grace maried to George Selye. | Anne 3 daughter. |

---

## Holland.

ARMS. *Azure, a lion rampant quardant between four crosses patté argent.*

Robert Holland, gentleman.═

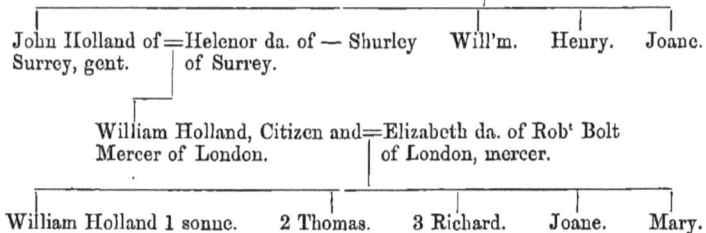

| | | | |
|---|---|---|---|
| John Holland of═Helenor da. of — Shurley Surrey, gent.    of Surrey. | Will'm. | Henry. | Joane. |

William Holland, Citizen and═Elizabeth da. of Rob't Bolt
Mercer of London.     of London, mercer.

| | | | |
|---|---|---|---|
| William Holland 1 sonne. | 2 Thomas. | 3 Richard. | Joane. | Mary. |

---

## Lee.

ARMS. *Argent, on a fess between three leopards' heads sable a crescent or.*

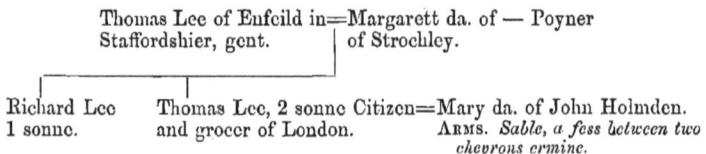

Thomas Lee of Enfeild in═Margarett da. of — Poyner
Staffordshier, gent.     of Strochley.

| | |
|---|---|
| Richard Lee 1 sonne. | Thomas Lee, 2 sonne Citizen═Mary da. of John Holmden. and grocer of London.    ARMS. *Sable, a fess between two chevrons ermine.* |

## Walton.

ARMS. *Argent, on a fleur-de-lis gules, a mullet or.*

Thomas Walton of Hamme in com. Som'sett gent.=

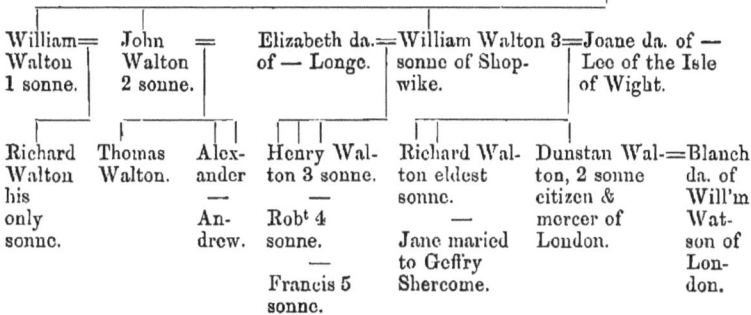

| | | | | | |
|---|---|---|---|---|---|
| William= Walton 1 sonne. | John = Walton 2 sonne. | | Elizabeth da.= of — Longe. | William Walton 3= sonne of Shop- wike. | Joane da. of — Lee of the Isle of Wight. |

| | | | | | |
|---|---|---|---|---|---|
| Richard Walton his only sonne. | Thomas Walton. | Alex- ander — An- drew. | Henry Wal- ton 3 sonne. — Rob't 4 sonne. — Francis 5 sonne. | Richard Wal- ton eldest sonne. — Jane maried to Geffry Shercome. | Dunstan Wal-=Blanch ton, 2 sonne da. of citizen & Will'm mercer of Wat- London. son of Lon- don. |

---

## Wilkynson.

ARMS. *Quarterly :—1 and 4. Gules, a fess vair between two unicorns courant or. 2. Ermine, on a chevron engrailed sable three roses argent. (GILBERD.) 3. Argent, a fess gules between three parrots vert beaked and collared of the second. (LOMLEY.)*

John Wilkynson of Gold- =Jane da. and heyre of John Gilberd sonne & heire of
hanger in com. Essex    Nicholas Gilberd and Elizabeth his wife da. and
gent.    heyre of Will'm Lomley 3 sonne to Rafe Lomley
    first Lo. Lomley.

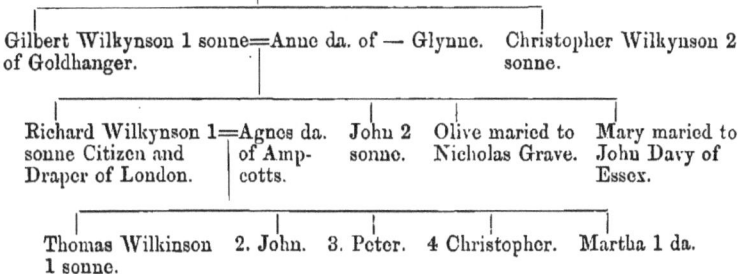

| | |
|---|---|
| Gilbert Wilkynson 1 sonne=Anne da. of — Glynne. of Goldhanger. | Christopher Wilkynson 2 sonne. |

| | | | |
|---|---|---|---|
| Richard Wilkynson 1=Agnes da. sonne Citizen and of Amp- Draper of London. cotts. | John 2 sonne. | Olive maried to Nicholas Grave. | Mary maried to John Davy of Essex. |

| | | | | |
|---|---|---|---|---|
| Thomas Wilkinson 1 sonne. | 2. John. | 3. Peter. | 4 Christopher. | Martha 1 da. |

I

## Dawbney.

ARMS. *Gules, five fusils conjoined in fess argent, on the centre one a fleur-de-lis sable.*

John Dawbney of London, gent.═Alice da. of — Edes of Warwickshier.

Oliver Dawbney of═Elizabeth da. of     Joane maried to — Higgins
London, gent.    | — Drayner.     of London.

Rowland Dawbney.        Anne.

## Dove.

ARMS. *Sable, a fess dancetté ermine between three doves argent, beaked and legged gules; in chief a crescent or for difference.*
CREST. *A dove argent, wings sable, charged with a crescent for difference.*

Henry Dove of Stradbroke in com. Suff. gent.═Alice da. of — Nowell.

| Christopher | Robert Dove 2═Lettice da. of | Joane maried | Eleonor maried to |
| Dove, eldest | sonne Citizen | Nicholas | to Nicholas | Nicholas Hari- |
| sonne. | and March[t] | Bull of Lon- | H. | son of London. |
| | Taylor of | don. | | |
| | London. | | | |

Robert Dove 1 sonne.   2. John.   3. Henry.   4 Thomas.   5 Richard.

## Astry.

ARMS. *Barry wavy of six argent and azure, on a chief gules three bezants; a crescent for difference.*

Sᵣ Rafe Astrey, Knight, he maried to his 1 wife,═Margarett da. of — Hill.
Margery by whom he had no issue.

William Astry 1 sonne═Isabell da. of — Pigott of Bechington    Rafe Astry 2
and heyre.         | in com. Buck.                sonne.

| Thomas | Francis Astry 2═Elizabeth da. of Oliver | Elizabeth maried to |
| Astry 1 | sonne of Lon- | Smyth of London. | William Bugby of Hun- |
| sonne. | don, gent. | | tingdonshire. |

## Sowdeak.

ARMS. *Argent, on a fess dancetté gules an annulet or, from the sinister chief an arm issuing from clouds proper vested gules, touching in the chief point a heart of the last between two spear-heads sable, pointing inwards.*

CREST. *A dexter arm erect, couped at the elbow, vested gules, charged with an annulet or, cuffed with a frill argent, holding in the hand proper a heart of the first.*

William Sowdeak al's Sowtheak of Comberland.=Isabell da. of — Hutton.

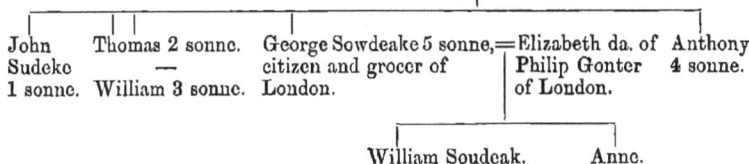

| John Sudeke 1 sonne. | Thomas 2 sonne. — William 3 sonne. | George Sowdeake 5 sonne,=Elizabeth da. of citizen and grocer of London. | Philip Gonter of London. | Anthony 4 sonne. |

William Soudeak.     Anne.

## Heton.

ARMS. *Quarterly:—1 and 4. Argent, on a bend engrailed sable three bulls' heads couped of the field. 2 and 3. Argent, a Moor's head sable banded round the forehead of the first and second, between three fleurs-de-lis of the second.*

CREST. *Out of a ducal coronet gules, a bull's head argent.*

Bryan Heton of Lancashier.=Catarine da. of Thurston Anderton of Anderton.

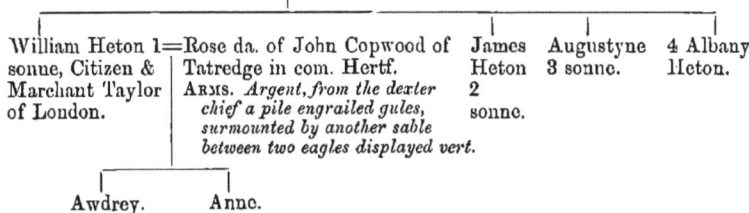

| William Heton 1=Rose da. of John Copwood of sonne, Citizen & Tatredge in com. Hertf. Marchant Taylor ARMS. *Argent, from the dexter of London. chief a pile engrailed gules, surmounted by another sable between two eagles displayed vert.* | James Heton 2 sonne. | Augustyne 3 sonne. | 4 Albany Heton. |

Awdrey.     Anne.

## Barney.

ARMS. *Per pale azure and gules, a cross engrailed argent.*

John Barney of Reedham in=Margaret da. of Sir Roger Wentworth Norff.     of Coddam in Essex.

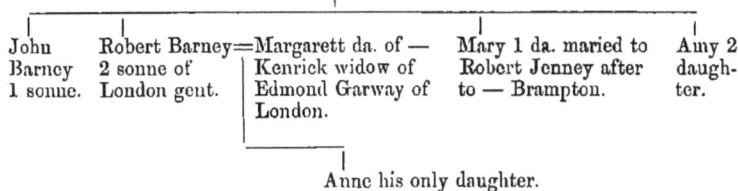

| John Barney 1 sonne. | Robert Barney=Margarett da. of — 2 sonne of Kenrick widow of London gent. Edmond Garway of London. | Mary 1 da. maried to Robert Jenney after to — Brampton. | Amy 2 daughter. |

Anne his only daughter.

## Sanforde.

ARMS. *Argent, on a chevron between three doves sable, beaked and legged gules, an annulet or.*

Hugh Sanforde of Miluerton in com. Somersetsh. gent.=Maud his wife.

William Sanforde.=Agnes da. of Nicolas Rodway.

John Sanforde=Agnes da. of — Bonvile.

Anne da. of . . . =John Sanforde of Mil-=Margarett da. of Andrew Harlewyn
                   uerton.                of Colompton.

| Richard Sanforde. | James. — Alice. | Bartholomew 1 sonne. — Xpofer 2 sonne unto whome the land was conveyed. | 3. George. — 4 Henry. | Edward Sanforde 5 sonne Citizen & Marchantaylor of London. | =Marg'y da. of Giles Bruges of London Draper. | Baldwyn Sanforde 6 sonne. |
|---|---|---|---|---|---|---|

## Benne.

ARMS. *Argent, a fess dancetté gules between three dragons' heads erased vert.*
CREST. *A tiger statant ermine, ducally gorged and tufted or.*

Henry Benne of Saffron Walden in Essex.=

John Benne, yeoman of the Crowne= — da. of John Burrell of Wormley in
to King H. 7 and H. 8.            com. Hertf. Sergeant at Armes to K. H.
                                  7 and H. 8.

Thomas Benne   Robert Benne=Elizabeth da. and coheyre   Mercy first maried
1 sonne ob.    Citizen and  of Reignold Woodeson.        to . . . Robson after
s. p.          Ironmonger   ARMS. *Or, on a cross azure,* to . . . Derick.
               of London.       *pierced of the field, four*
                                *eagles displayed or.*

Anthony Benne.        John Benne.

# Longe.

ARMS. *Sable semé of crosses crosslet, a lion rampant argent within a bordure engrailed or.*

Simon Longe of London, gent.=Alice da. of — Huglett who maried the da. of — Kirkby of Essex.

Morris Longe Citizen & Clothworker of=Margaret da. of —    Mary maried to London he maried to his 2nd wife Jane    Hamond of Hart-    Wm Allen of Lon-da. of — Mayto of Abingdon.    fordshire his 1 wife.    don Alderman.

| John Longe 1 sonne. | 2. Anthony. 3. Willm. 4. Robt. | 5. George. 6. Morris. 7. Simon. | Alice. Mary. Anne. | Margaret. | Elizab. | Juditha. |

# Lason.

ARMS. *Per pale argent and sable, a chevron counterchanged, in chief an annulet or.*
CREST. *Out of clouds proper two arms embowed vested ermine, holding in the hands proper a sun in splendour or.*

William Lason of Osworth in the= — da. of John Hedworth Bishoprick of Durham.    of Harverton.

| Thomas Lason 1 sonne. | 2 Robert. 3 Willm. 4 John. | George Lason=Catarine da. of Robert 5 sonne of    Smarte of London. London, gent.    ARMS. *Argent, on a bend engrailed azure between two demi-greyhounds couped sable gutté d'or, three thistles vert seeded or.* | Rowland 6 sonne. |

Alice.      Agnes.      Catharine.

# Okeover.

ARMS. *Ermine, on a chief gules three bezants, the centre one charged with a mullet sable.*
CREST. *An oak-tree vert, acorned or.*

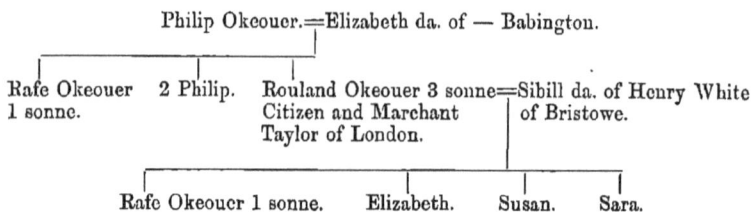

Philip Okeouer.=Elizabeth da. of — Babington.

Rafe Okeouer     2 Philip.     Rouland Okeouer 3 sonne=Sibill da. of Henry White
1 sonne.                       Citizen and Marchant    of Bristowe.
                               Taylor of London.

Rafe Okeouer 1 sonne.     Elizabeth.     Susan.     Sara.

---

# Wanton.

ARMS. *Quarterly :—1 and 4. Argent, a chevron and in dexter chief an annulet sable.
    2. Ermine, a chevron engrailed between three griffins' heads erased gules.
    (LAXTON.)   3. Ermine, a chief indented gules.*
CREST. *An eagle preying on a dove proper.*

Thomas Wanton citizen and=Joane da. of John Laxton and heyre to S$^r$ W$^m$
Grocer of London.         Laxton brother of the sayd John.

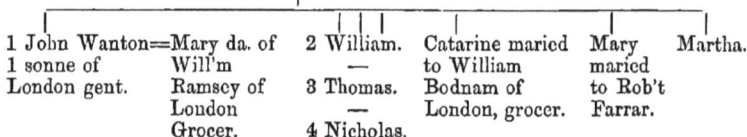

1 John Wanton=Mary da. of    2 William.    Catarine maried    Mary       Martha.
1 sonne of    Will'm         —             to William         maried
London gent.  Ramsey of      3 Thomas.     Bodnam of          to Rob't
              London         —             London, grocer.    Farrar.
              Grocer.        4 Nicholas.

---

# Browne.

ARMS. *Gules, a griffin segreant or, a chief indented per fess of the second and ermine.*
CREST. *A mountain-cat ermine.*

John Browne of Rayly in com. Essex gent.=Agnes his wife.

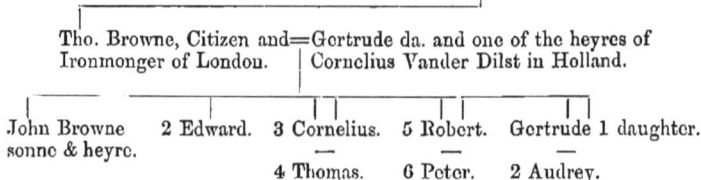

Tho. Browne, Citizen and=Gertrude da. and one of the heyres of
Ironmonger of London.    Cornelius Vander Dilst in Holland.

John Browne    2 Edward.    3 Cornelius.    5 Robert.    Gertrude 1 daughter.
sonne & heyre.              —               —
               4 Thomas.   6 Peter.    2 Audrey.

# Wayer.

ARMS. *Or, two lions passant in pale azure within a bordure gules charged with eight martlets or.*

Bethsaba daughter=Thomas Wayer of London gent, Citizen= — da. of — Bluett
of — Cortes. | and Fishmonger of London. | 1 wife.

Richard Wayer 3 Isack.  Susan.  Eliz.  Thomas Wayre al's Waycre
2 sonne.  —  —  —  his eldest sonne.
4 Jacob.  Anne.  Bethsaba.

# Pattenson.

ARMS. *Argent, on a fess sable three fleurs-de-lis or.*
CREST. *Out of a ducal coronet proper a horse's head sable semé of plates.*

John Pattenson of Cheriburton in com.=Ellen da. of Bryan Chew
Ebor gent. | Knight.

Joh'nes Patenson  Brianus Patenson Citizen=Alice da. of William Kede of litle
1 sonne.  and Vintonner of London | holme al's of the Wood in the
2 sonne. | County of York.

Brian Patenson 1 sonne.  2 Robert.  Christian.  Prudence.

# Backhouse.

ARMS. *Per saltire azure and or, a saltire couped ermine.*
CREST. *An eagle vert, armed or, wings closed, preying upon a snake proper.*

Thomas Backhouse of Whitrige in=Elen da. of John Parkyn of Hartloo
com. Cumbr. gent. | in Cumb'land.

Nicholas Backhowse gent.=Anne da. of Tho. Curson of Croxall in Darbishier.
ARMS. *Quarterly:*—1 *and* 4. *Azure, on a bend between
two lions rampant argent, three popinjays vert, beaked
and legged gules.* 2. *Vairy or and gules, on a chief
sable, three horseshoes argent.* 3. *Gules, on a bend
argent three martlets sable.*

Samuel Backhouse  2. Miles.  Sara maried to Nicholas Fuller Coun-  Mary.
1 sonne.  —  sellor at lawe, alias Fulwer.
3. Rowland.

## 𝖂arner.

ARMS. *Quarterly :—1 and 4. Or, a chevron between three boars' heads couped sable.*
*2. Or, a fess dancetté sable, in chief a martlet gules.* (VAVASOR.) *3. Per pale*
*or and argent, three crescents ermines.*
CREST. *A horse's head erased per fess ermine and gules.*

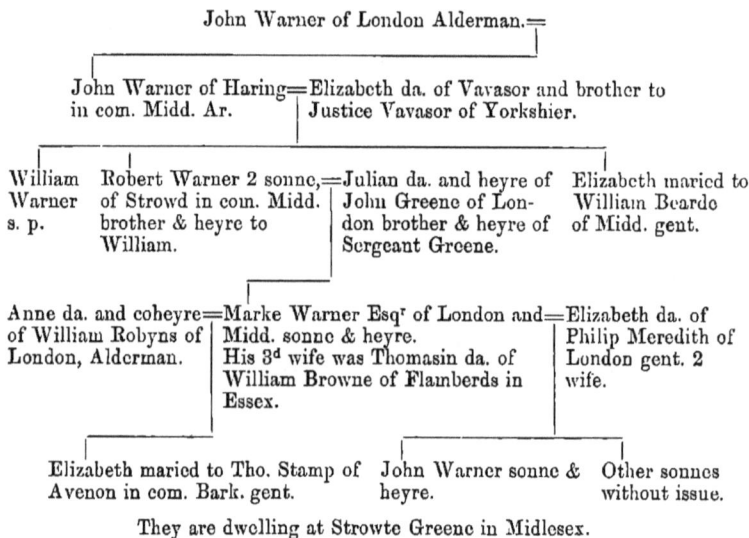

John Warner of London Alderman.=

John Warner of Haring=Elizabeth da. of Vavasor and brother to
in com. Midd. Ar. | Justice Vavasor of Yorkshier.

William | Robert Warner 2 sonne,=Julian da. and heyre of | Elizabeth maried to
Warner | of Strowd in com. Midd. | John Greene of Lon- | William Beardo
s. p. | brother & heyre to | don brother & heyre of | of Midd. gent.
| William. | Sergeant Greene.

Anne da. and coheyre=Marke Warner Esqʳ of London and=Elizabeth da. of
of William Robyns of | Midd. sonne & heyre. | Philip Meredith of
London, Alderman. | His 3ᵈ wife was Thomasin da. of | London gent. 2
| William Browne of Flamberds in | wife.
| Essex.

Elizabeth maried to Tho. Stamp of | John Warner sonne & | Other sonnes
Avenon in com. Bark. gent. | heyre. | without issue.

They are dwelling at Strowte Greene in Midlesex.

## 𝕺ffley.

ARMS. *Argent, on a cross flory azure between four Cornish choughs sable, beaked*
*and legs gules, a lion passant guardant or.*
CREST. *A demi-lion rampant per pale or and azure, collar counterchanged, holding*
*in his paws an olive branch vert fructed or.*

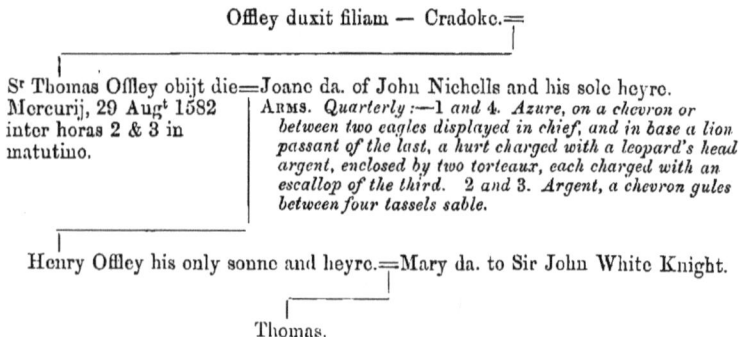

Offley duxit filiam — Cradoke.=

Sʳ Thomas Offley obijt die=Joane da. of John Nichells and his sole heyre.
Mercurij, 29 Augᵗ 1582 | ARMS. *Quarterly :—1 and 4. Azure, on a chevron or*
inter horas 2 & 3 in | *between two eagles displayed in chief, and in base a lion*
matutino. | *passant of the last, a hurt charged with a leopard's head*
| *argent, enclosed by two torteaux, each charged with an*
| *escallop of the third. 2 and 3. Argent, a chevron gules*
| *between four tassels sable.*

Henry Offley his only sonne and heyre.=Mary da. to Sir John White Knight.

Thomas.

## Anes.

ARMS. *Argent, a lion rampant guardant gules within an orle of torteaux.*

George Anes of Valiodely in Spayne=Elizabeth da. of — Rotriges.
al's Vallodolid.

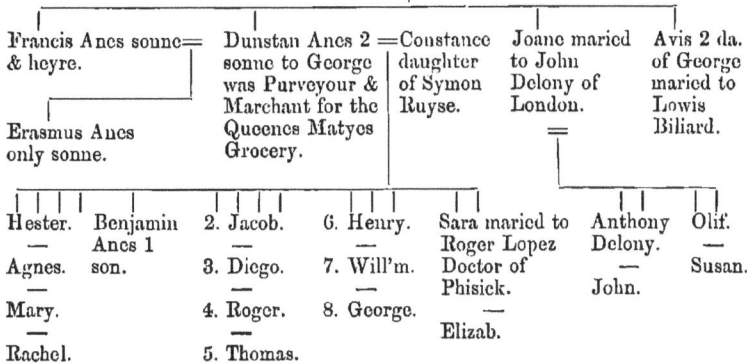

| Francis Anes sonne= & heyre. | Dunstan Anes 2 =Constance sonne to George daughter was Purveyour & of Symon Marchant for the Ruyse. Queenes Matyes Grocery. | Joane maried to John Delony of London. | Avis 2 da. of George maried to Lowis Biliard. |

Erasmus Anes only sonne.

| Hester. | Benjamin Anes 1 son. | 2. Jacob. | 6. Henry. | Sara maried to Roger Lopez Doctor of Phisick. | Anthony Delony. | Olif. |
| — Agnes. | | 3. Diego. | 7. Will'm. | | — John. | — Susan. |
| — Mary. | | 4. Roger. | 8. George. | — Elizab. | | |
| — Rachel. | | 5. Thomas. | | | | |

## Bradbery.

ARMS. *Quarterly:—1 and 4. Sable, a chevron ermine between three round buckles argent. 2 and 3. Argent, a chevron between three chess rooks sable.*
CREST. *A demi-dove argent, fretty gules, holding in the beak a slip of barberry vert, fructed of the first.*

John Bradbury of Lichfield Gent.=Elizabeth da. of — Leftchilde.

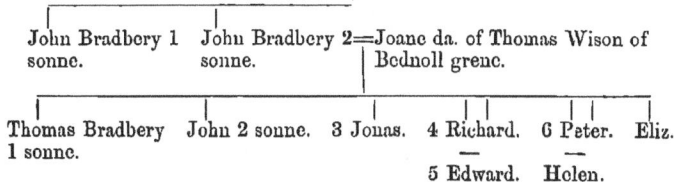

| John Bradbery 1 sonne. | John Bradbery 2=Joane da. of Thomas Wison of Bednoll grene. |

| Thomas Bradbery 1 sonne. | John 2 sonne. | 3 Jonas. | 4 Richard. | 6 Peter. | Eliz. |
| | | | 5 Edward. | Helen. | |

## Rigges.

ARMS. *Gules, a fess between three water-spaniels argent, each holding in their mouths a bird bolt in bend or.*
CREST. *A water-spaniel argent, holding in its mouth a bird bolt or.*

K

# Cooper.

ARMS. *Argent, three martlets gules, on a chief engrailed of the second as many annulets or.*
CREST. *A lion's gamb erect or, holding a branch vert, fructed gules.*

Richard Cooper of Madeley in com. Salop.=

Editha da. of — Smith=Richard Cooper=Sibill da. of William Hopkyns of
of London.        of London gent.  Haubery in Worcestershire.

Lionell Cooper his sonne & heyre.

# Philipson.

ARMS. *Sable, a chevron ermine between three bats expanded argent.*
CREST. *A horse's head or, crined sable, holding in his mouth an oak branch vert, acorned or.*

Mathew Philipson of Kendall in com.=Anne da. of — Boothe of
Ebor gent.               Lincolnshier.

Robert Philipson=Margaret da. of John   Mark 2   Elizabeth maried to John
sonne & heyre of  Parker of London.     sonne.   Coxston of London.
London, gent.     ARMS. *Argent, on a fess*
              *between three pheons sable, as many bezants.*

# Nicolls.

ARMS. *Azure, a fess between three lions' heads erased or.*
CREST. *A tiger sejant ermine.*

Christian da. of=John Nicolls of London, gent at this=Ellen da. of James Holt
— Thomson 1   present controller of the workes at   of Stubley in Com. Lanc.
wife.       London Bridge and all other lands   ARMS. *Argent, on a bend*
         and revenues of the same, & in     *engrailed sable, three*
         charge for provision of Corne for   *fleurs-de-lis of the field.*
         the City of London.

Mary maried to Francis     Elizabeth maried to Edmond Cook of Lizenes
Garrad.             in Kent, gent.

## Sares.

ARMS. *Gules, a chevron argent between three Saracens' heads couped at the shoulders or, eyes proper.*
CREST. *A goat's head erased argent, armed or.*

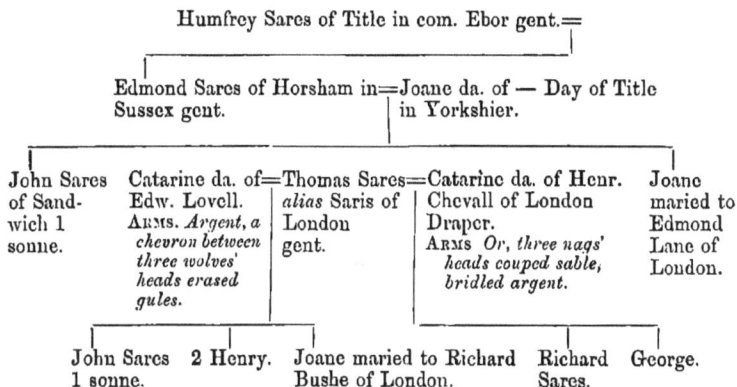

Humfrey Sares of Title in com. Ebor gent.=

Edmond Sares of Horsham in=Joane da. of — Day of Title
Sussex gent.          in Yorkshier.

| John Sares of Sandwich 1 sonne. | Catarine da. of=Edw. Lovell. ARMS. *Argent, a chevron between three wolves' heads erased gules.* | Thomas Sares= *alias* Saris of London gent. | Catarine da. of Henr. Chevall of London Draper. ARMS *Or, three nags' heads couped sable, bridled argent.* | Joane maried to Edmond Lane of London. |

| John Sares 1 sonne. | 2 Henry. | Joane maried to Richard Bushe of London. | Richard Sares. | George. |

---

## Grange.

ARMS. *Azure, a chevron between three lions rampant or, on a chief of the second three escallops gules within a bordure compony of the second and last.*
CREST. *A griffin's head erased sable, beaked and eared or, charged with three bezants.*

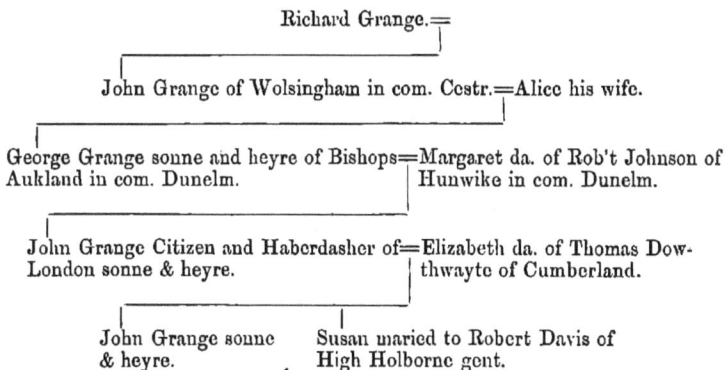

Richard Grange.=

John Grange of Wolsingham in com. Cestr.=Alice his wife.

George Grange sonne and heyre of Bishops=Margaret da. of Rob't Johnson of
Aukland in com. Dunelm.       Hunwike in com. Dunelm.

John Grange Citizen and Haberdasher of=Elizabeth da. of Thomas Dow-
London sonne & heyre.       thwayte of Cumberland.

| John Grange sonne & heyre. | Susan maried to Robert Davis of High Holborne gent. |

---

# Ramsey.

ARMS. *Sable, a chevron ermine between three rams' heads erased argent, horned or.*
CREST. *A griffin's head erased per fess indented argent and sable, in base guttée d'or.*

John Ramsey of Eatonbridge in com. Cantij.=

| Will'mus 1 filius. | Mary da. to William Dale of Bristowe marchant s. p. | =S<sup>r</sup> Thomas Ramsey Sheriff of London A° 1568, after mayor s. p. | =Alice da. of Bevis Lee of Stafford-shier s. p. ARMS. *Argent, on a fess between three leopards' heads sable, a crescent or.* | Richard 3 sonne s. p. | Jone mar. to — New-man. — Elizabeth Ramsey. |

# Birde.

ARMS. *Quarterly :—1 and 4. Per pale or and argent, an eagle displayed sable. 2 and 3. Quarterly gules and or, in the first and fourth three fleurs-de-lis argent, over all a trefoil slipped azure.* (MASSIE.)
CREST. *A griffin's head erased bendy of six sable and argent.*

Randolf Birde of Yowley in com. Cestr.=da. of — Marbury.

Richard Bird sonne & heyre.=da. of — Davenport of Henbury.

Richard Bird sonne & heyre.=da. & heyre of — Doddon.

John Byrde of Yowley.=da. of William Chantrell of the Bache.

John Birde of Yowley.=Anne da. of John Delves Esq.

| John Bird 1 sonne. | Thomas Bird= 2 sonne. | Richard Bird 3 sonne. |

| Roger Birde 1 sonne ob. s. p. | Hugh Byrde=Alice da. of — Horton 2 sonne.        of Wilteshier. | John Bird 3 sonne. |

| Mary maried to Robert Burges of Wilteshier. | William Byrde Esq.=Mirabell da. Customer owtward     of Tho. to the Queenes     Rivett of Mat<sup>y</sup> for London.  Suffolk. | Alice maried to — Isher of Wiltshier. | Anne maried to John Warder of Wiltshier. |

Thomas Byrde 1 son.    2 William.    3 Walter.    4 Francis.

# Smyth.

ARMS. *Per pale or and azure, a chevron argent between three lions counterchanged.*
CREST. *A tiger's head erased argent pelletté, collared sable bezanté and chained or.*

Thomas Smyth Esq. Collector of the Queens=Alice da. of S^r Andrew Judde of
Mat^s Subsidy for tonage and Poundage & | London, Knight.
farmor for the Custome and subsidy | ARMS. *Quarterly:—1 and 4. Gules, a*
inwards. | *fess ragulé between three boars'*
| *heads couped argent. 2 and 3.*
| *Azure, three lions rampant within a*
| *bordure argent.*

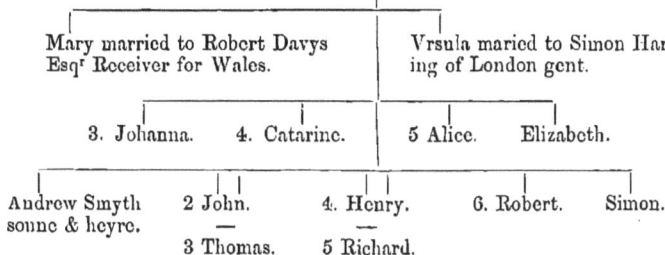

Mary married to Robert Davys | Vrsula maried to Simon Hard-
Esq^r Receiver for Wales. | ing of London gent.

3. Johanna.    4. Catarine.    5 Alice.    Elizabeth.

Andrew Smyth    2 John.    4. Henry.    6. Robert.    Simon.
sonne & heyre.      3 Thomas.    5 Richard.

---

# Billingsley.

ARMS. *Argent, within a cross voided between four lions rampant five estoiles sable.*

William Billingsley of London gent,=Elizabeth da. of
Citizen and Haberdasher of London. | — Hardy.

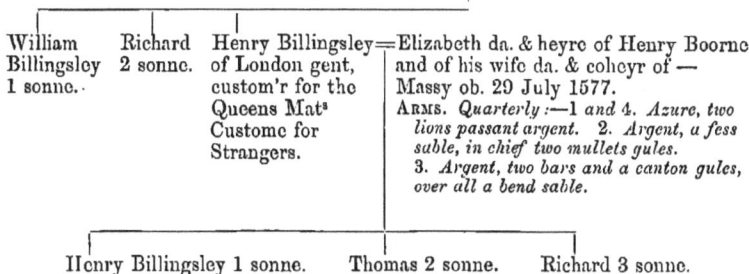

William    Richard    Henry Billingsley=Elizabeth da. & heyre of Henry Boorne
Billingsley   2 sonne.   of London gent, | and of his wife da. & coheyr of —
1 sonne.          custom'r for the | Massy ob. 29 July 1577.
               Queens Mat^s | ARMS. *Quarterly:—1 and 4. Azure, two*
               Custome for | *lions passant argent. 2. Argent, a fess*
               Strangers. | *sable, in chief two mullets gules.*
                                    | *3. Argent, two bars and a canton gules,*
                                    | *over all a bend sable.*

Henry Billingsley 1 sonne.      Thomas 2 sonne.      Richard 3 sonne.

# Grey.

ARMS. *Barry of six argent and azure, on a bend gules a rose of the field.*
CREST. *On a mount vert a bear argent.*

Richard Grey gent. descended of a younger═
brother of — Grey of Rotherfeild.

Walter Grey his son and heir.

Margery da. of═Richard Grey of London, gent.═Dorothy da. of Simon Lynch of
— Henley of │ Searcher for the Queenes │ Cranbrok in Kent.
Cornwall. │ Mat^yes Custome. │ ARMS. *Sable, three leopards rampant argent, spotted of the field.*

Mathew    Humfrey 5.    Helena.    William Grey    2 Henry.    Margarett maried to
Grey                                sonne and      —           Will^m Langhorne
4 sonne.                            heyre.         3 Edmond.   of London, drap.

# Young.

James Young of Charnes in com. Staff.═Anne da. of — Perivs of Shropshier.

John         Richard Yonng    3 Humfry.    Margery        Dorothy        Anne maried to
Young        of London                     mar. to —      mar. to        Roger Hinton
1 sonne.     Packer to the                 Dickons        — Man-         of Richardon
             Strangers.                     of com.        waring of      in Shropshier.
             ═                              Bedf.          Pever
             Joane da. of — Croston                        Cheshier.
             of Westchester.

Francis Younge sonne & heyre.

# Kayle *sive* Kele.

ARMS. *Quarterly embattled argent and sable, in first quarter a mullet counterchanged.*
CREST. *A wyvern argent, wings or.*

# Philipps.

ARMS. *Or, a lion rampant sable, ducally gorged and chained of the field.*
CREST. *A lion sejant sable, ducally gorged and chained or.*

Robert Philipps of — =Elizabetha daughter of — Mampas.

John Philipps sonne and heyre.=Joane da. of Richard Clayton.

William Philipps of London gent.=Joane da. of Tho. Houghton.
one of the Queens Mat⁵ Cus-     ARMS. *Sable, three bars argent,*
tomers for the Wooll.     *in dexter chief a bezant.*

# Lovell.

ARMS. *Argent, a chevron sable between three foxes' heads erased gules.*

Henry Lovell of Skelton in com. Ebor. gent.=Margarett daughter of — Gay
a second brother of the same howse.     of Leicestershier.

Thomas Lovell of London gent.=Margarett da. of — Pikering
one of the Queenes Ma^tys     of Hasellwood in Yorkshire.
Customers for Wooll.

Elizabeth 1 daughter.     Elizabeth 2 daughter.     Margaret.

# Wycliff.

ARMS. *Or, three bars azure.*
CREST. *A dragon's head argent.*

# Woore.

ARMS. *Gules, a bend argent fretty sable, between three griffins' heads erased or.*
CREST. *Out of a ducal coronet or, a demi-heraldic panther argent spotted vert, gules
and azure, holding in his paw a branch of laurel slipped vert fructed gules.*

Richard Woore of London.=

# Thwaytes.

[ARMS. *Argent, a cross sable, fretty of the field, in the first quarter a fleur-de-lis gules.*
CREST. *A game-cock proper, beaked and wattled gules, charged on the breast with a fleur-de-lis of the last.*
Granted by Wm. Dethick and Wm. Camden, Clarenceux, 1597.]

Thomas Thwaytes of Yorkshier.=

William Thwaytes of Cheping Wickham in com. Buck.=

William Thwaytes Citizen and Alderman of London (1597).

# Turfeet of London.

ARMS. *Argent, an orle sable within an orle of eight martlets gules.*
CREST. *On a ducal coronet argent a stag trippant proper.*

# Jackman.

ARMS. *Per saltire argent and sable, in chief and in base an eagle displayed counterchanged.*
CREST. *A griffin's head erased sable, gutty or.*

Edward Jackman, Alderman=Ann da. of Humphrey Pakington.
and Sheriff of London A°
D^ni 1564.

ARMS. *Quarterly:—1 and 4. Per chevron sable and argent in chief three mullets or, in base as many garbs gules. 2. Argent, on a fess between six martlets gules three quatrefoils of the field.* (WASHBOURNE.) *3. Argent, on a bend azure three martlets or.* (HARDING.)

John Jackman, eldest sonne & heyre,=Jane 2 da. of Richard Lambart, of London, grocer.   Alderman of London.

Edward Jackman of Hacton in the Liberty=Margaret da. of S^r Edward Sulliard of Haveringe in the County of Essex.   of Fleminges in com. Essex K^t.

2. John Jackman.=Jane da. of Peter Bettesworth of Com. Sussex.   1 Edward.   Anne m. Robert Poleby.

## 𝔙illett *alias* 𝔙iolet.

ARMS. *Argent, on a chevron gules three towers triple-towered of the field, on a canton azure a fleur-de-lis or.*
CREST. *A tiger's head erased ermine, ducally gorged and tufted or.*

Henry Villett alias Violett of London and now of Kent.

---

## 𝔔uarles.

John Quarles Esq$^r$, Citizen & Draper of London, died 12 day of November 1577.

---

## 𝔗edcastle.

ARMS. *Quarterly :—*1 and 4. *Argent, three pales sable, on a chief azure as many lions' heads erased or.* 2 and 3. *Argent, on a fess gules three crescents or between two cotices wavy sable ; impaling vert a chevron between three roses or, a chief indented ermine.* (MAY.)
concess. p' R. Cook Clarenceux, A° D'ni 1590.

John Tedcastle of London sup'stes 1590.═Elizabeth May his wife.

---

## 𝔥arison.

ARMS. *Quarterly :—*1 and 4. *Gules, an eagle displayed and a chief or.* 2 and 3. *Sable, a chevron between three dexter hands fessways clenched argent, erased gules.*
CREST. *A snake vert entwined round a broken column or.*

-- Harison of London Citizen.═ — his wife da. of —.
ARMS. *Argent, a chevron ermines between three martlets sable.*
(EDWARDES or JARVIS?).

---

L

# Colston.

John Colston of Corby in com. Lincoln.=

Robert Colston of Corby=Catherine da. and coh.
in com. Lincoln. | of — Mallorye.

1 Michael=    Gabriell Colston=Alice da. to    Elizabeth maried    Alice mar. to
Colston.     of London     Michael     to Wᵐ Flecher     Richard Brookes
        Fishmonger.     Foxe of     of London     of London,
                London      salter ob. s. p.     Sopeboyler.
                Grocer.

Judith    Sir Mi-=3 Elizabeth=Henrye    Judith    Ralphe=Alice    2 Anne
twise     chael    Colston.    Parvish    died     Col-    Piers    maried
maried    Hickes          of Lon-    s. p.     ston of   da. to    to Sir
in      2 husb.         don              Essex.   — Piers    Thomas
Sussex.              Marchᵗ                  linen     Lowe
                      1 husbᵈ.                    draper    Knight
                                               of      Alder-
                                               London.   man of
                                                          London.

Will'm    Elizabeth    5 Elizabeth    Anne.    Gabriel Parvish.    Gabriell    Alice
Hickes.    Hickes.     mar. to —     —      —            Colston    maried
—              Trott.     Ellen.    George, s. p.     now     to —
John                       —                     living.    Bell, a
Hickes.                  Mary.    Henry Parvish                mar-
                                maried in Venice.               chant of
                                3 sonne.                   London.
                                —
                                Thomas Parvish
                                4 sonne.

1 John    3 Gabriel    Anne mar.    Elizabeth    Christopher    Alice      Margery
Brookes   Brookes.    to —      Brook     Brookes     Brookes    maried in
&                 Thornell    mar. to    2 sonne.     maried     Essex.
4 Henry            of Sand-    Tristram               Rob't      —
s. p.              wich.      Basford               Throny-    Catherine
                      marchant &             ton of    maried to
                      haberdasher           London    Nicolas
                      of London.            haber-     Thompson
                                            dasher &   Sopeboyler.
                                            marchant.

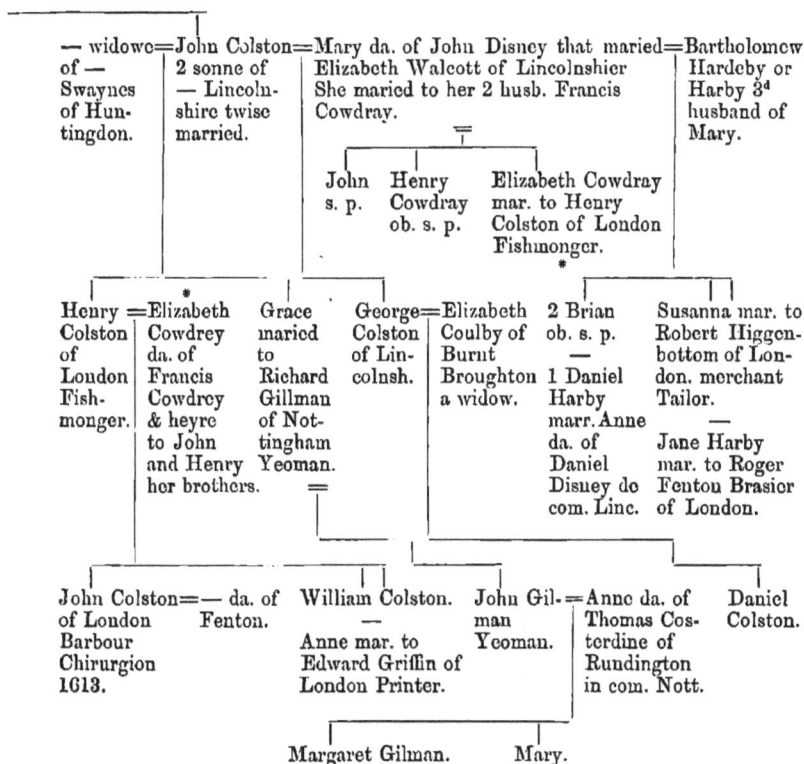

```
— widowe=John Colston=Mary da. of John Disney that maried=Bartholomew
of —      2 sonne of    Elizabeth Walcott of Lincolnshier   Hardeby or
Swaynes   — Lincoln-   She maried to her 2 husb. Francis     Harby 3ᵈ
of Hun-   shire twise  Cowdray.                              husband of
tingdon.  married.                                           Mary.
```

```
                        John   Henry      Elizabeth Cowdray
                        s. p.  Cowdray    mar. to Henry
                               ob. s. p.  Colston of London
                                          Fishmonger.
```

```
Henry =Elizabeth   Grace      George=Elizabeth   2 Brian        Susanna mar. to
Colston Cowdrey    maried     Colston Coulby of   ob. s. p.      Robert Higgen-
of      da. of     to         of Lin- Burnt       —              bottom of Lon-
London  Francis    Richard    colnsh. Broughton   1 Daniel       don. merchant
Fish-   Cowdrey    Gillman            a widow.    Harby          Tailor.
monger. & heyre    of Not-                        marr. Anne     —
        to John    tingham                        da. of         Jane Harby
        and Henry  Yeoman.                        Daniel         mar. to Roger
        her brothers.                             Disney de      Fenton Brasior
                                                  com. Linc.     of London.
```

```
John Colston=— da. of   William Colston.   John Gil-=Anne da. of    Daniel
of London    Fenton.    —                  man       Thomas Cos-    Colston.
Barbour                 Anne mar. to       Yeoman.   terdine of
Chirurgion              Edward Griffin of             Rundington
1613.                   London Printer.              in com. Nott.
```

```
              Margaret Gilman.          Mary.
```

## 𝔉𝔦𝔣𝔢𝔦𝔩𝔡 *alias* 𝔏𝔬𝔴𝔢.

ARMS. *Quarterly :—1 and 4. Per fess vert and argent a pale counterchanged, on the first three acorns or. (FIFIELD.) 2 and 3. Argent, six ogresses, three, two, and one, a mullet gules. (LACY.)*

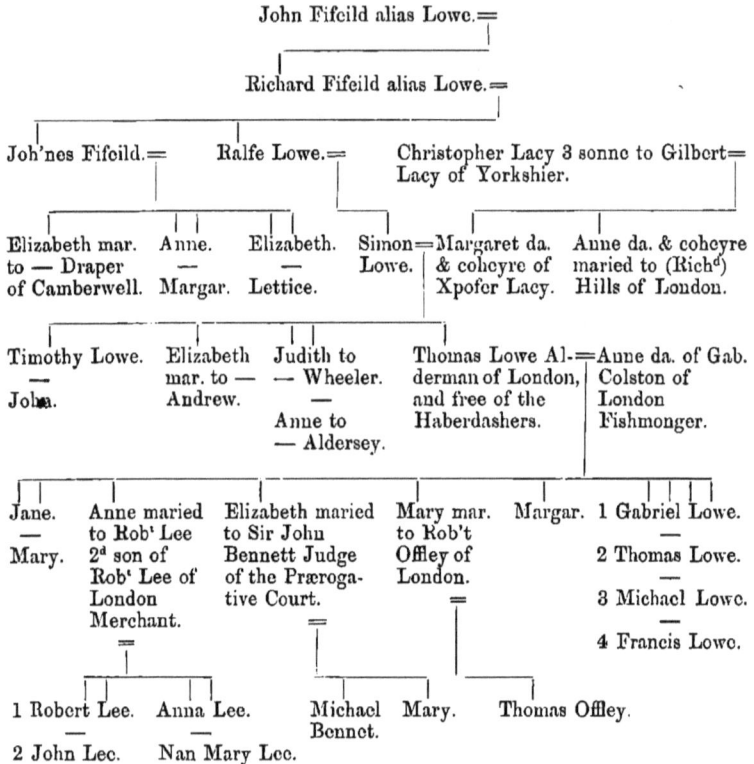

John Fifeild alias Lowe.=

Richard Fifeild alias Lowe. =

| Joh'nes Fifeild.= | Ralfe Lowe.= | Christopher Lacy 3 sonne to Gilbert= Lacy of Yorkshier. | |

| Elizabeth mar. to — Draper of Camberwell. | Anne. — Margar. | Elizabeth. — Lettice. | Simon= Lowe. | Margaret da. & coheyre of Xpofer Lacy. | Anne da. & coheyre maried to (Rich^d) Hills of London. |

| Timothy Lowe. — John. | Elizabeth mar. to — Andrew. | Judith to — Wheeler. — Anne to — Aldersey. | Thomas Lowe Al-= derman of London, and free of the Haberdashers. | Anne da. of Gab. Colston of London Fishmonger. |

| Jane. — Mary. | Anne maried to Rob^t Lee 2^d son of Rob^t Lee of London Merchant. = | Elizabeth maried to Sir John Bennett Judge of the Prærogative Court. = | Mary mar. to Rob't Offley of London. = | Margar. | 1 Gabriel Lowe. — 2 Thomas Lowe. — 3 Michael Lowe. — 4 Francis Lowe. |

| 1 Robert Lee. — 2 John Lee. | Anna Lee. — Nan Mary Lee. | Michael Bennet. | Mary. | Thomas Offley. |

# Sutton.

ARMS. *Or, a lion rampant vert, a canton ermine.*
CREST. *A demi-lion rampant vert.*

William Sutton sonne of — Sutton of Ediall in com. Staffordiæ.=

John Sutton of Henley sup' Thames=Elizabeth da. of — Tailor of
in com. Oxon. | Ediall in com. Staff.

Richard Sutton of London Esquier=Elizabeth da. of George Fishe
now Auditor. 1612. | of Ayott Montfichett.

— filia et hæres nupta Jacobo Altham milit. filio Baronis de S'c'cio.

# Shaa.

Flam civis Londinensis.=
ARMS. *Argent, a fess engrailed*
*between six cinquefoils sable.*

Joh'nes Shaa miles maior London 1 Marit.=Margareta filia et hæres
ARMS. *Argent, a chevron between three* | renupta Joh'i Rayns-
*lozenges ermines.* | ford militi.

Thomas= | Etheldreda ux. | Juliana ux. | Edmundus Shaa=Lora filia Rogeri
Shaa. | Will'mi Ayloff | Ricardi | of Horndon on | Wentworth
| de Bretaignes | Fowler de | the Hill in | Militis.
| in Essex, qui | Ricott in | Essex.
| ob. 1517. | com. Oxon.

Thomas Shaa | Alicia filia & hæres | — ux. Will[i] Browne filij
filius & hæres | nupta Will'o Poley | Joh'is Browne maioris
Thomæ. | de Boxted in Suff. | London: & militis.
=

Johannes Poley de Boxted.

# Haydon.

ARMS. *Quarterly of six :*—1. *Argent, three bars gemelles azure, on a chief gules a bar dancetté or.* (HAYDON.) 2. *Ermine, three battle-axes (sable), in chief a crescent.* (WEEKES.) 3. *Argent, two chevrons within a bordure engrailed gules.* (KYMBER.) 4. *Ermine, two surgeons' flams in saltire gules.* (TIDER-LEIGH.) 5. *Argent, two chevrons azure within a bordure engrailed gules, a martlet (sable) for difference.* 6. *Argent, ten torteaux, four, three, two, and one, a label of three points azure.* (BABINGTON.)
CREST. *A lion argent, seizing on a bull courant sable.*
MOTTO. *" Ferme en foy."*

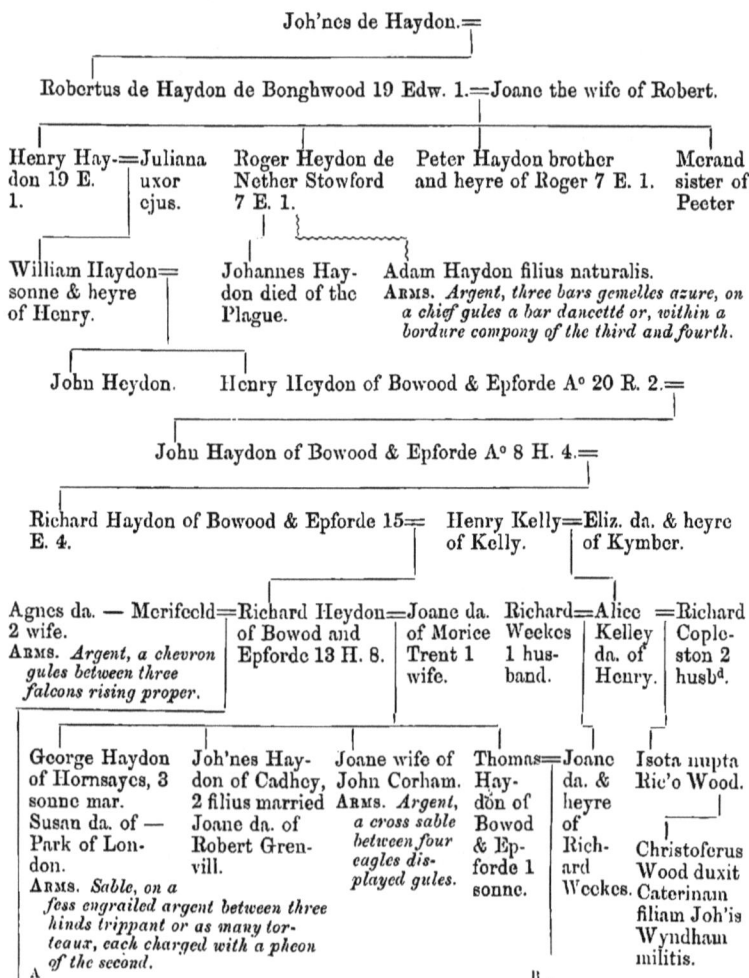

Joh'nes de Haydon.=

Robertus de Haydon de Bonghwood 19 Edw. 1.=Joane the wife of Robert.

Henry Hay-=Juliana　　Roger Heydon de　　Peter Haydon brother　　Merand
don 19 E.　uxor　　Nether Stowford　　and heyre of Roger 7 E. 1.　sister of
1.　　ejus.　　7 E. 1.　　　　　　　　　　　　Peeter

William Haydon=　　Johannes Hay-　Adam Haydon filius naturalis.
sonne & heyre　　don died of the　ARMS. *Argent, three bars gemelles azure, on*
of Henry.　　Plague.　　*a chief gules a bar dancetté or, within a*
　　　　　　　　　　*bordure compony of the third and fourth.*

John Heydon.　　Henry Heydon of Bowood & Epforde A° 20 R. 2.=

John Haydon of Bowood & Epforde A° 8 H. 4.=

Richard Haydon of Bowood & Epforde 15=　Henry Kelly=Eliz. da. & heyre
E. 4.　　　　　　　　　　　　　　of Kelly.　of Kymber.

Agnes da. — Merifeeld=Richard Heydon=Joane da.　Richard=Alice　=Richard
2 wife.　　　of Bowod and　of Morice　Weekes　Kelley　Cople-
ARMS. *Argent, a chevron*　Epforde 13 H. 8.　Trent 1　1 hus-　da. of　ston 2
*gules between three*　　　　　wife.　band.　Henry.　husb{d}.
*falcons rising proper.*

George Haydon　Joh'nes Hay-　Joane wife of　Thomas=Joane　Isota nupta
of Hornsayes, 3　don of Cadhey,　John Corham.　Hay-　da. &　Ric'o Wood.
sonne mar.　2 filius married　ARMS. *Argent,*　don of　heyre
Susan da. of —　Joane da. of　*a cross sable*　& Ep-　of
Park of Lon-　Robert Gren-　*between four*　forde 1　Rich-　Christoferus
don.　vill.　*eagles dis-*　sonne.　ard　Wood duxit
ARMS. *Sable, on a*　　　*played gules.*　　Weekes. Caterinam
*fess engrailed argent between three*　　　　　　filiam Joh'is
*hinds trippant or as many tor-*　　　　　　Wyndham
*teaux, each charged with a pheon*　　　　　　militis.
*of the second.*

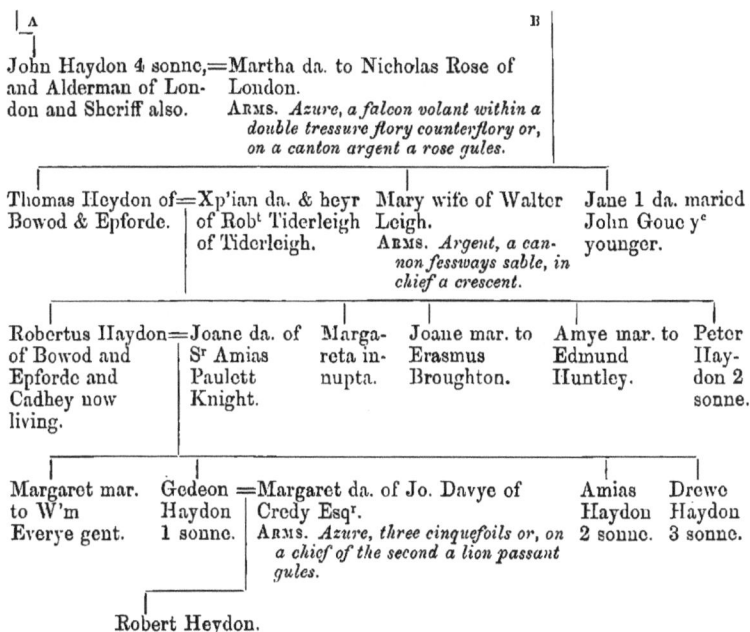

| A | B |
|---|---|

John Haydon 4 sonne,=Martha da. to Nicholas Rose of
and Alderman of Lon- London.
don and Sheriff also. ARMS. *Azure, a falcon volant within a*
*double tressure flory counterflory or,*
*on a canton argent a rose gules.*

Thomas Heydon of=Xp'ian da. & heyr Mary wife of Walter Jane 1 da. maried
Bowod & Epforde. of Rob$^t$ Tiderleigh Leigh. John Goue y$^e$
of Tiderleigh. ARMS. *Argent, a can-* younger.
*non fessways sable, in*
*chief a crescent.*

Robertus Haydon=Joane da. of Marga- Joane mar. to Amye mar. to Peter
of Bowod and S$^r$ Amias reta in- Erasmus Edmund Hay-
Epforde and Paulett nupta. Broughton. Huntley. don 2
Cadhey now Knight. sonne.
living.

Margaret mar. Gedeon =Margaret da. of Jo. Davye of Amias Drewe
to W'm Haydon Credy Esq$^r$. Haydon Haydon
Everye gent. 1 sonne. ARMS. *Azure, three cinquefoils or, on* 2 sonne. 3 sonne.
*a chief of the second a lion passant*
*gules.*

Robert Heydon.

# Bruges.

ARMS. *Argent, on a cross sable a leopard's head, and in chief a crescent or.*

Johannes Bruges, civis & Aldermannus=Agnes filia Thomæ
London miles 1520, A$^o$ 12 H. 8. Ayloff de Essex.

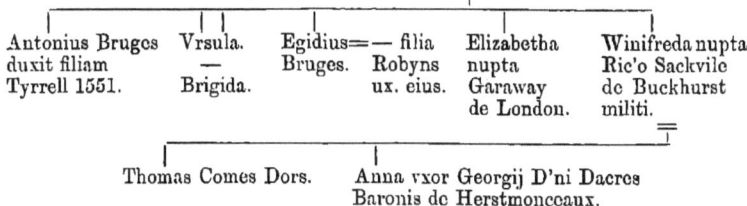

Antonius Bruges Vrsula. Egidius=— filia Elizabetha Winifreda nupta
duxit filiam — Bruges. Robyns nupta Ric'o Sackvile
Tyrrell 1551. Brigida. ux. eius. Garaway de Buckhurst
de London. militi.

Thomas Comes Dors. Anna vxor Georgij D'ni Dacres
Baronis de Herstmonceaux.

# Peacock.

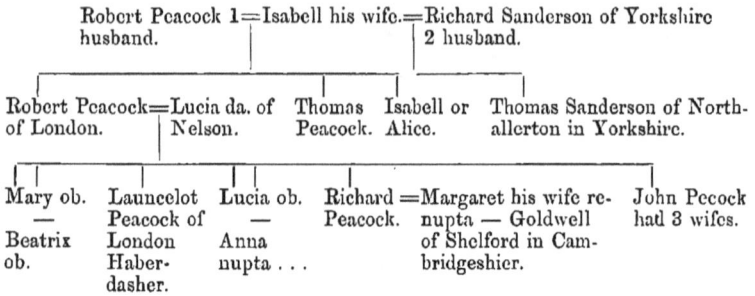

Robert Peacock 1=Isabell his wife.=Richard Sanderson of Yorkshire
husband.                        2 husband.

Robert Peacock=Lucia da. of   Thomas   Isabell or   Thomas Sanderson of North-
of London.      Nelson.        Peacock.  Alice.      allerton in Yorkshire.

Mary ob.   Launcelot   Lucia ob.   Richard =Margaret his wife re-   John Pecock
—          Peacock of  —           Peacock.  nupta — Goldwell        had 3 wifes.
Beatrix    London      Anna                 of Shelford in Cam-
ob.        Haber-      nupta . . .          bridgeshier.
           dasher.

# Sotherton.

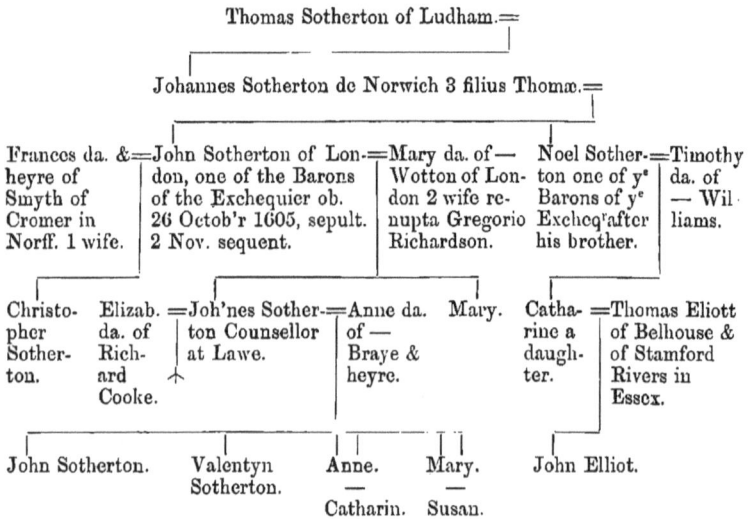

Arms. *Argent, a fess and in chief two crescents gules.*

Thomas Sotherton of Ludham.=

Johannes Sotherton de Norwich 3 filius Thomæ.=

Frances da. &=John Sotherton of Lon-=Mary da. of —   Noel Sother-=Timothy
heyre of      don, one of the Barons   Wotton of Lon-  ton one of y˙   da. of
Smyth of      of the Exchequier ob.    don 2 wife re-  Barons of yᵉ    — Wil-
Cromer in     26 Octob'r 1605, sepult. nupta Gregorio  Exchcq'after    liams.
Norff. 1 wife. 2 Nov. sequent.         Richardson.     his brother.

Christo-   Elizab. =Joh'nes Sother-=Anne da.   Mary.   Catha- =Thomas Eliott
pher       da. of   ton Counsellor   of —              rine a  of Belhouse &
Sother-    Rich-    at Lawe.         Braye &           daugh-  of Stamford
ton.       ard      ⅄                heyre.            ter.    Rivers in
           Cooke.                                              Essex.

John Sotherton.   Valentyn      Anne.   Mary.   John Elliot.
                  Sotherton.    —       —
                                Catharin. Susan.

# Porke.

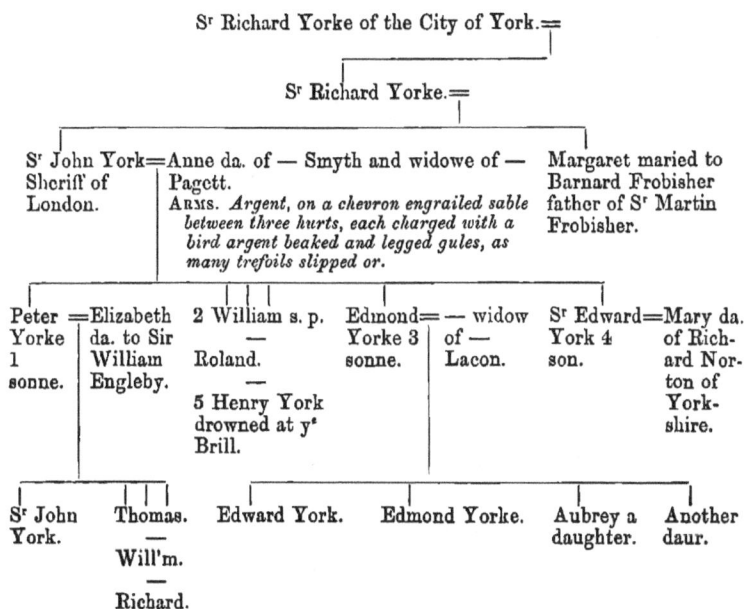

Sᴿ Richard Yorke of the City of York.=

Sᴿ Richard Yorke.=

| | | |
|---|---|---|
| Sᴿ John York=Anne da. of — Smyth and widowe of — | Margaret maried to |
| Sheriff of ⎪ Pagett. | Barnard Frobisher |
| London. ⎪ Aʀᴍs. *Argent, on a chevron engrailed sable* | father of Sᴿ Martin |
| *between three hurts, each charged with a* | Frobisher. |
| *bird argent beaked and legged gules, as* | |
| *many trefoils slipped or.* | |

| Peter =Elizabeth | 2 William s. p. | Edmond= — widow | Sᴿ Edward=Mary da. |
|---|---|---|---|
| Yorke ⎪ da. to Sir | — | Yorke 3 ⎪ of — | York 4 ⎪ of Rich- |
| 1 ⎪ William | Roland. | sonne. ⎪ Lacon. | son. ⎪ ard Nor- |
| sonne. ⎪ Engleby. | — | | ⎪ ton of |
| | 5 Henry York | | ⎪ York- |
| | drowned at yᵉ | | ⎪ shire. |
| | Brill. | | |

| Sᴿ John | Thomas. | Edward York. | Edmond Yorke. | Aubrey a | Another |
|---|---|---|---|---|---|
| York. | — | | | daughter. | daur. |
| | Will'm. | | | | |
| | — | | | | |
| | Richard. | | | | |

# Essex.

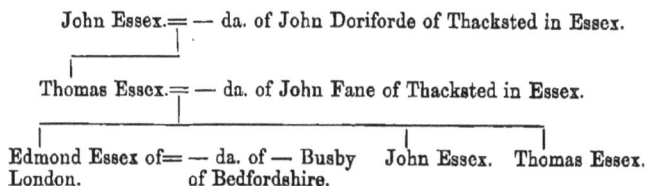

John Essex.= — da. of John Doriforde of Thacksted in Essex.

Thomas Essex.= — da. of John Fane of Thacksted in Essex.

| | | |
|---|---|---|
| Edmond Essex of= — da. of — Busby | John Essex. | Thomas Essex. |
| London. of Bedfordshire. | | |

## Freare.

John Freare of Balsome in= — da. of — Barnatt of Kent.
the County of Cambridge. | ARMS. *Argent, a saltire between four leopards'*
*heads sable.*

John Freare Doctor in Phisik and=Vrsula da. of Robert Castell of
Phisition to Queene Mary. | East Hatley in Cambridgeshier.

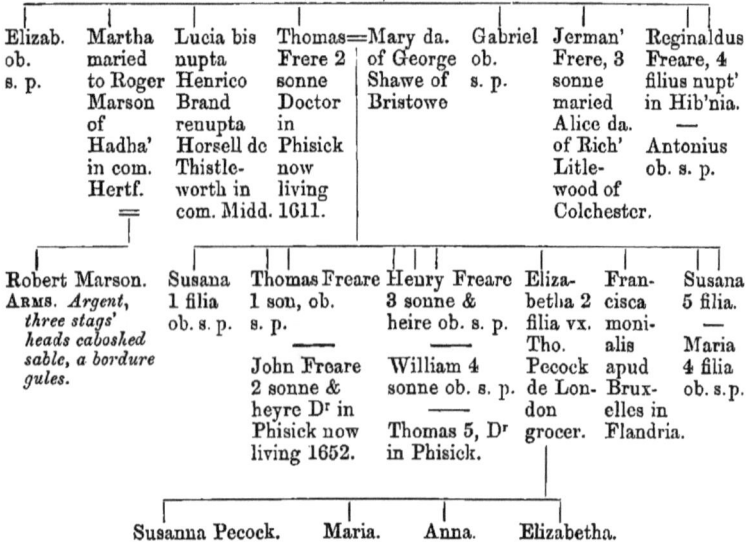

| Elizab. ob. s. p. | Martha maried to Roger Marson of Hadha' in com. Hertf. = | Lucia bis nupta Henrico Brand renupta Horsell de Thistleworth in com. Midd. | Thomas=Mary da. Frere 2 sonne Doctor in Phisick now living 1611. | of George Shawe of Bristowe | Gabriel ob. s. p. | Jerman' Frere, 3 sonne maried Alice da. of Rich' Litlewood of Colchester. | Reginaldus Freare, 4 filius nupt' in Hib'nia. — Antonius ob. s. p. |

| Robert Marson. ARMS. *Argent, three stags' heads caboshed sable, a bordure gules.* | Susana 1 filia ob. s. p. | Thomas Freare 1 son, ob. s. p. ——— John Freare 2 sonne & heyre D^r in Phisick now living 1652. | Henry Freare 3 sonne & heire ob. s. p. ——— William 4 sonne ob. s. p. Thomas 5, D^r in Phisick. | Elizabetha 2 filia vx. Tho. Pecock de London grocer. | Francisca monialis apud Bruxelles in Flandria. | Susana 5 filia. — Maria 4 filia ob. s. p. |

Susanna Pecock.     Maria.     Anna.     Elizabetha.

## Bullock.

Thomas Bullock.=

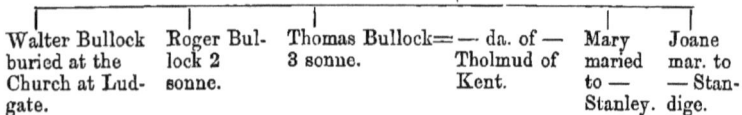

| Walter Bullock buried at the Church at Ludgate. | Roger Bullock 2 sonne. | Thomas Bullock= 3 sonne. | — da. of — Tholmud of Kent. | Mary maried to — Stanley. | Joane mar. to — Standige. |

# Cowper.

ARMS. *Argent, on a bend engrailed between two lions rampant sable three plates.*
CREST. *A lion rampant sable, holding paleways a tilting spear argent.*

John Couper Esq^r Seriant of Lawe borne at Horlye in y^e County of Surrey 1539 maried Julian da. of Cuthbert Blackden Esq. w^ch John was Seariantt at lawe but one yeare and half & died the 15 of March 1590, being of the age of 51 yeares and lieth buried at Cappell in Surrey.

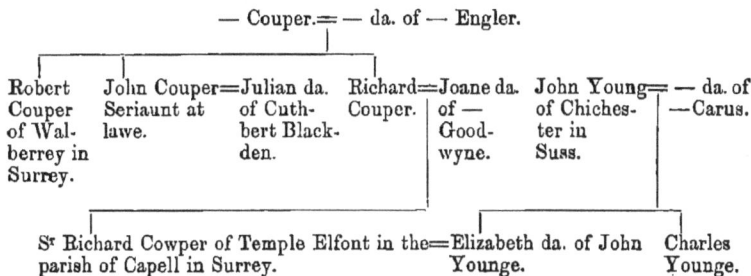

— Couper.= — da. of — Engler.

| Robert Couper of Walberrey in Surrey. | John Couper= Seriaunt at lawe. | Julian da. of Cuthbert Blackden. | Richard= Couper. | Joane da. of — Goodwyne. | John Young= of Chichester in Suss. | — da. of —Carus. |

S^r Richard Cowper of Temple Elfont in the= parish of Capell in Surrey. =Elizabeth da. of John Younge.  Charles Younge.

---

# Harborne.

ARMS. *Gules, on a fess or between three bezants a lion passant sable, a crescent for difference.*
CREST. *A bezant between two lions' gambs sable.*

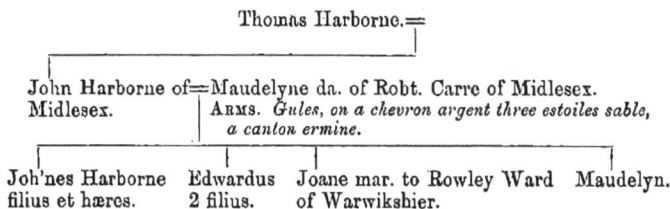

Thomas Harborne.=

| John Harborne of= Midlesex. | Maudelyne da. of Robt. Carre of Midlesex. ARMS. *Gules, on a chevron argent three estoiles sable, a canton ermine.* |

| Joh'nes Harborne filius et hæres. | Edwardus 2 filius. | Joane mar. to Rowley Ward of Warwikshier. | Maudelyn. |

William Harborne of Yarmouth (bears), *Gules, on a fess or between three bezants a lion passant sable, impaling argent on a chief vert a cross tau between two mullets or.* (DRURY.)
CREST. *On a cap of maintenance sable, turned up ermine, an eagle displayed or.*

## Stile.

ARMS. *Sable, a fess or fretty of the field between three fleurs-de-lis within a bordure of the second.*

Sir Guy Wolston Knᵗ 19 E. IV. =

Margareta filia & cohæres nupta = Guidoni Sabcote militi.

John Stile of Langley in yᵉ p'ish of = Eliz. da. & coheyre of Sir Guy Wolston qui fuit sup'stes 19 E. 4.
Beckenham in Kent.   ARMS. *Quarterly :—1 and 4, Argent, a wolf passant sable. 2. Argent, three turnstiles sable, a mullet for difference. 3. Argent, on a chevron sable between three rams' heads erased azure, as many billets or.*

Eliz. f. Geo. = Sᵗ Humfrey Stile of = Briget da. to Sᵗ    Brigida nupta Edm'o    Florencia nupta    Eliz. vx. Joh'is    Anna vx. Jo. Brough-
Peryn vx.   Langley sonne & heyre,   Tho. Baldry    Kempe civi London   Rob'to Robin-    Stile renupta    ton militis; renupta
2.    Kᵗ p. H. 8 at his going   maior of Lon-    nato in Suff.     son de Boston.    Jacobo Yar-    Joh'ni com. Bedford.
    to Bullen.     don.        ford militi.

Edwardus   Maria vx.   Edmond sonne & = Mary da. of   Joh'nes   Oliver Stile = Susan da. of — Bull   Nicholas = Gertrude da. of —   Edw.
ob. iuve-   Xpoferi   heyre of Sᵗ Hum-   John    s. p.     2 sonne and    of London.    Stile 4   Bright of London.   s. p.
nis s. p.   Meade   frey Stile Knight   Berney of      Sheriff of    ARMS. *Argent, on a*   sonne   ARMS. *Sable, on a bend*
    de com.   & Briget his wife,   Redham in     London.     *canton sable a lion's*   Sheriff of   *between three mullets two*
    Warr.    of Langley.    Norf. Esq.    ‖        *head erased or.*    London.   *and one argent, three crosses*
                          Julian da. of                                  *crosslet fitché of the field.*
                          — Barnes
                          2 wife.

Anna vx.   Anne sole da. of = William Stile = Mary da. of Sir   Edmond = Catherina da. of Jo.   Margareta    Thomas Stile    Maria vx.
Georgii   John Eversfield   son & heyre   Robᵗ Clark    Stile.    Scott of Kent.    vx. Georgii    of Watring-    Simonis
Franklyn   of Sussex Esq.   of Langley.   Baron of yᵉ       ARMS. *Three catherine*   Needham de   bury in     Law-
de com.   ali' Ersfeild.      Exchequer.        *wheels within a bor-*   com. Hertf.   Kent. =    rence
Bedf.                                           *dure engrailed.*

Humfridus Stile.

A     B     c

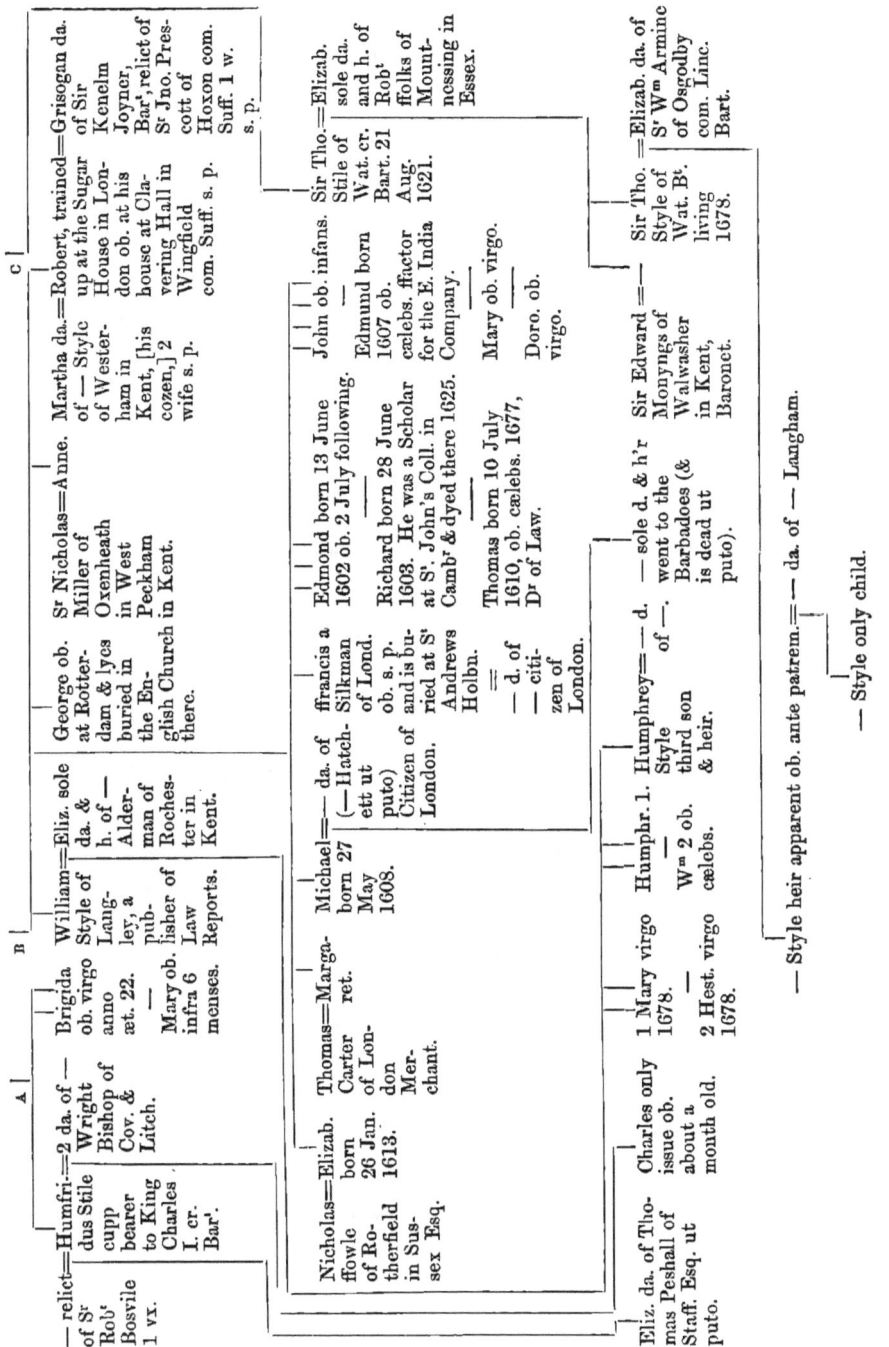

A | B | C |

— relict of Sr Robt Bosvile 1 vx. = Humfridus Stile cupp bearer to King Charles I. cr. Bart. = 2 da. of Wright Bishop of Cov. & Litch.

Brigida ob. virgo anno æt. 22. — Mary ob. infra 6 menses.

William Style of Langley, a publisher of Law Reports. = Eliz. sole da. & h. of — Alderman of Rochester in Kent.

George ob. at Rotterdam & lyes buried in the English Church there.

Sr Nicholas Miller of Oxenheath in West Peckham in Kent. = Anne.

Martha da. of — Style of Westerham in Kent, [his cozen,] 2 wife s. p. = Robert, trained up at the Sugar House in London ob. at his house at Clavering Hall in Wingfield com. Suff. s. p. = Grisogan da. of Sir Kenelm Joyner, Bart, relict of Sr Jno. Prescott of Hoxon com. Suff. 1 w. s. p.

Nicholas ffowle of Rotherfield in Sussex Esqr. = Elizab. born 26 Jan. 1613.

Thomas Carter of London Merchant. = Marga-ret.

Michael born 27 May 1608. = — da. of (— Hatchett ut puto) Citizen of London.

ffrancis a Silkman of Lond. ob. s. p. and is buried at St Andrews Holbn. == — d. of — citizen of London.

Edmond born 13 June 1602 ob. 2 July following.

Richard born 28 June 1603. He was a Scholar at St. John's Coll. in Cambr & dyed there 1625.

Thomas born 10 July 1610, ob. cælebs. 1677, Dr of Law.

John ob. infans.

Edmund born 1607 ob. cælebs. ffactor for the E. India Company.

Mary ob. virgo.

Doro. ob. virgo.

Sir Tho. Stile of Wat. cr. Bart. 21 Aug. 1621. = Elizab. sole da. and h. of Robt ffolks of Mountnessing in Essex.

Eliz. da. of Thomas Peshall of Staff. Esq. ut puto.

Charles only issue ob. about a month old.

1 Mary virgo 1678. — 2 Hest. virgo 1678.

Humphr. 1. Wm 2 ob. cælebs.

Humphrey Style third son & heir. = — d. of —.

— sole d. & h'r went to the Barbadoes (& is dead ut puto).

Sir Edward Monyngs of Walwasher in Kent, Baronet.

Sir Tho. Style of Wat. Bt living 1678. = Elizab. da. of Sr Wm Armine of Osgrolby com. Linc. Bart.

== Style heir apparent ob. ante patrem. == — da. of — Langham.

— Style only child.

# Harbye.

ARMS. *Gules, a fess dancetté ermine between ten billets argent, four in chief, three, two, and one in base, a mullet for difference.*

CREST. *A heron's head erased or, beaked sable, between two wings expanded of the last bezanté.*

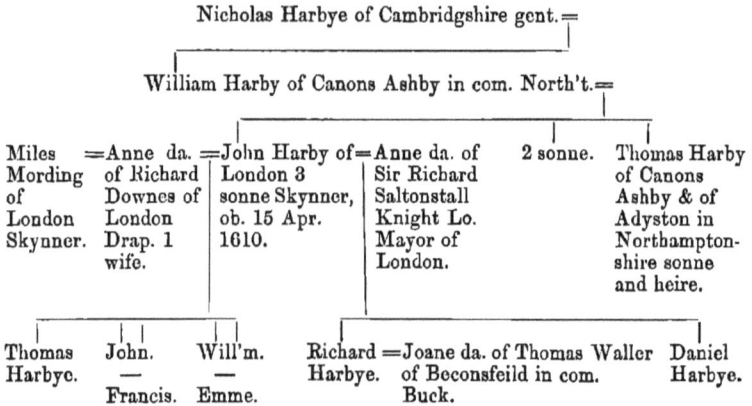

Nicholas Harbye of Cambridgshire gent. =

William Harby of Canons Ashby in com. North't. =

| Miles Mording of London Skynner. | =Anne da. of Richard Downes of London Drap. 1 wife. | =John Harby of London 3 sonne Skynner, ob. 15 Apr. 1610. | =Anne da. of Sir Richard Saltonstall Knight Lo. Mayor of London. | 2 sonne. | Thomas Harby of Canons Ashby & of Adyston in Northampton-shire sonne and heire. |

| Thomas Harbye. | John. — Francis. | Will'm. — Emme. | Richard Harbye. | =Joane da. of Thomas Waller of Beconsfeild in com. Buck. | Daniel Harbye. |

# Skynner.

ARMS. *(Argent), on a fess between three lures (gules) a lion passant (of the field).*

This epitaphe taken from of his toombe.

Here lieth yᵉ Corpes of Thomas Skynner late Citizen and Alderman of Londo' borne at Saffron Walden in Essex, who in the 65 yeare of his age, and on yᵉ 30 day of Dece'br Aᵒ Dni 1596 being then Lo. Mayor of this Citye dep'ted this life leauing behinde him 3 sonnes and 3 daughters.

| Blanch da. of Wᵐ Watson marchant to Q. Elizabeth. ARMS. *Or, a chevron engrailed azure between three martlets sable, on a chief of the second three crescents of the field.* | =Thomas Skynner= Lord Mayor of London had 3 wifes. | — daughter of — Thorne. ARMS. *Or, on a pile sable a griffin segreant of the field.* |

| Sʳ John Skynner. | Sʳ Thomas Skynner. | Richard died vn-maried. | Anne. | Julian. | Elizabeth marᵈ to Sʳ William Smyth. |

# Gardner.

ARMS. *Azure, a griffin passant or.*
CREST. *On a ducal coronet a lion passant guardant argent.*
ANOTHER. *A demi-unicorn crased, crowned and horned or, crined sable.*

William Gardenor of Hartfordshier.=Eliz. daughter of — Michell his wife.

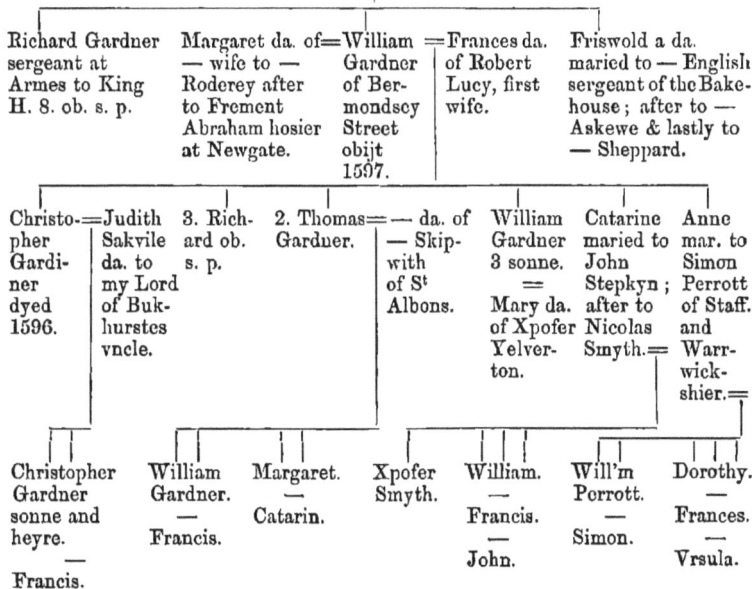

| Richard Gardner sergeant at Armes to King H. 8. ob. s. p. | Margaret da. of — wife to — Roderey after to Fremcnt Abraham hosier at Newgate. | =William Gardncr of Ber- mondscy Street obijt 1597. | =Frances da. of Robert Lucy, first wife. | Friswold a da. maried to — English sergeant of the Bake- house; after to — Askewe & lastly to — Sheppard. |

| Christo- pher Gardi- ner dyed 1596. | =Judith Sakvile da. to my Lord of Buk- hurstes vncle. | 3. Rich- ard ob. s. p. | 2. Thomas= Gardner. | =— da. of — Skip- with of Sᵗ Albons. | William Gardner 3 sonne. = Mary da. of Xpofer Yelver- ton. | Catarine maried to John Stepkyn; after to Nicolas Smyth.= | Anne mar. to Simon Perrott of Staff. and Warr- wick- shier.= |

| Christopher Gardner sonne and heyre. — Francis. | William Gardner. — Francis. | Margaret. — Catarin. | Xpofer Smyth. | William. — Francis. — John. | Will'm Porrott. — Simon. | Dorothy. — Frances. — Vrsula. |

---

# Baron.

ARMS. *Per fess azure and gules, two lions passant guardant argent, collared counter- changed.*

Concess. præfato Thomæ p' Rob. Cook Clarenceux post mortem in funere vtenda et suis in p'petuum.

| Anna filia Thomæ Aphowell de= Com. Monmouth in Wallia. ARMS. *Argent, a lion rampant sable debruised by a fess engrailed gules.* | =Thomas Baron alias Barne de= Alborough hache in p'ochia de Barking in Essex died at his howse in London 29 Junii 1573 & buried at Barking in Essex. | =Anna filia Rob'ti Brokesby de comitatu Lin- colniæ vxor prima. |

| Paulus Baron 3 filius. | Thomas Baron filius et hæres æt. 28 annor. | Barthus Baron ob. s. p. | Anna. |

# Romney.

ARMS. *Azure, on a bend cotised argent three escallops gules.*

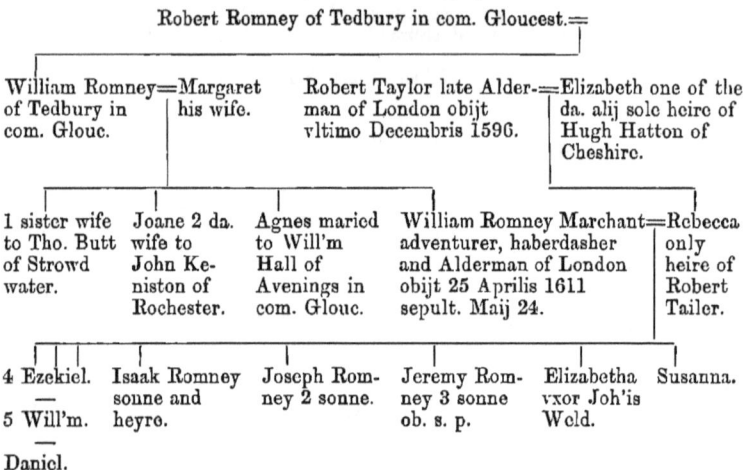

Robert Romney of Tedbury in com. Gloucest.=

| | | |
|---|---|---|
| William Romney=Margaret<br>of Tedbury in    his wife.<br>com. Glouc. | Robert Taylor late Alder-=Elizabeth one of the<br>man of London obijt    da. alij solc heire of<br>vltimo Decembris 1596.    Hugh Hatton of<br>    Cheshire. | |

| 1 sister wife<br>to Tho. Butt<br>of Strowd<br>water. | Joane 2 da.<br>wife to<br>John Ke-<br>niston of<br>Rochester. | Agnes maried<br>to Will'm<br>Hall of<br>Avenings in<br>com. Glouc. | William Romney Marchant=Rebecca<br>adventurer, haberdasher    only<br>and Alderman of London    heire of<br>obijt 25 Aprilis 1611    Robert<br>sepult. Maij 24.    Tailor. |
|---|---|---|---|

| 4 Ezekiel.<br>—<br>5 Will'm.<br>—<br>Daniel. | Isaak Romney<br>sonne and<br>heyre. | Joseph Rom-<br>ney 2 sonne. | Jeremy Rom-<br>ney 3 sonne<br>ob. s. p. | Elizabetha<br>vxor Joh'is<br>Weld. | Susanna. |
|---|---|---|---|---|---|

# Barnham.

ARMS. *Quarterly* :—1 *and* 4. *Sable, a cross engrailed between four crescents argent.*
2 *and* 3. *Azure, a pheon argent.* (BRADBRIDGE.)

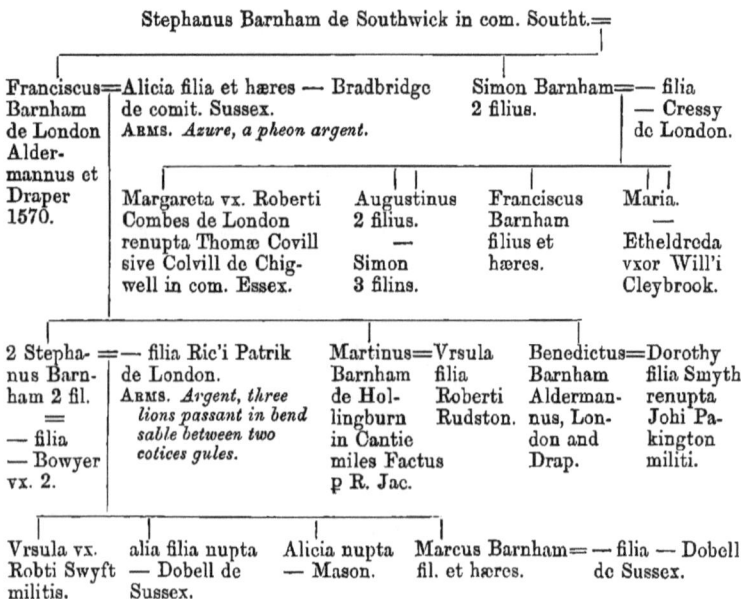

Stephanus Barnham de Southwick in com. Southt.=

| | | |
|---|---|---|
| Franciscus=Alicia filia et hæres — Bradbridge<br>Barnham    de comit. Sussex.<br>de London    ARMS. *Azure, a pheon argent.*<br>Alder-<br>mannus et<br>Draper<br>1570. | | Simon Barnham=— filia<br>2 filius.    — Cressy<br>    de London. |

| Margareta vx. Roberti<br>Combes de London<br>renupta Thomæ Covill<br>sive Colvill de Chig-<br>well in com. Essex. | Augustinus<br>2 filius.<br>—<br>Simon<br>3 filins. | Franciscus<br>Barnham<br>filius et<br>hæres. | Maria.<br>—<br>Etheldreda<br>vxor Will'i<br>Cleybrook. |
|---|---|---|---|

| 2 Stepha- =— filia Ric'i Patrik<br>nus Barn-    de London.<br>ham 2 fil.    ARMS. *Argent, three*<br>=    *lions passant in bend*<br>— filia    *sable between two*<br>— Bowyer    *cotices gules.*<br>vx. 2. | Martinus=Vrsula<br>Barnham    filia<br>de Hol-    Roberti<br>lingburn    Rudston.<br>in Cantic<br>miles Factus<br>p R. Jac. | Benedictus=Dorothy<br>Barnham    filia Smyth<br>Alderman-    renupta<br>nus, Lon-    Johi Pa-<br>don and    kington<br>Drap.    militi. |
|---|---|---|

| Vrsula vx.<br>Robti Swyft<br>militis. | alia filia nupta<br>— Dobell de<br>Sussex. | Alicia nupta<br>— Mason. | Marcus Barnham=— filia — Dobell<br>fil. et hæres.    de Sussex. |
|---|---|---|---|

# Dene.

ARMS. *Gules, a lion sejant guardant or, on a chief argent three crescents of the field.*
CREST. *A demi-lion rampant guardant or, holding a crescent gules.*

Concess. p' W^m Dethik Garter & W^m Camden Clarenceux.

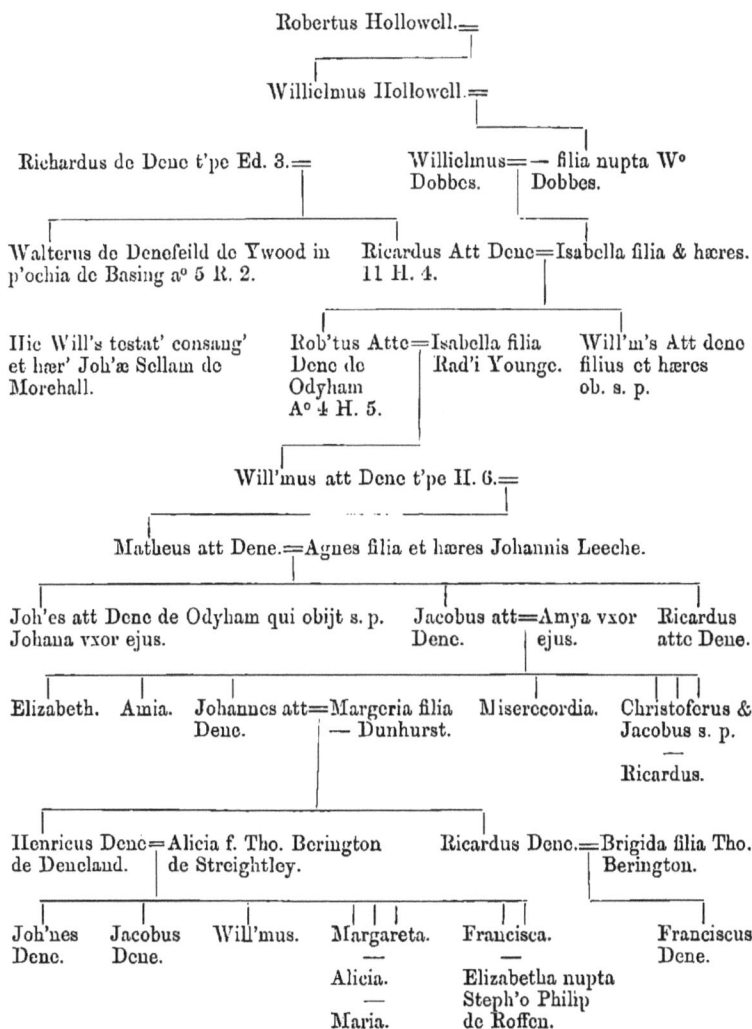

Robertus Hollowell.=

Willielmus Hollowell.=

Richardus de Dene t'pe Ed. 3.=       Willielmus=— filia nupta W°
                                      Dobbes.  |  Dobbes.

Walterus de Denefeild de Ywood in       Ricardus Att Dene=Isabella filia & hæres.
p'ochia de Basing a° 5 R. 2.            11 H. 4.

Hic Will's testat' consaug'       Rob'tus Atte=Isabella filia      Will'm's Att dene
et hær' Joh'æ Sellam de           Dene de  |  Rad'i Younge.        filius et hæres
Morehall.                         Odyham                           ob. s. p.
                                  A° 4 H. 5.

Will'mus att Dene t'pe H. 6.=

Matheus att Dene.=Agnes filia et hæres Johannis Leeche.

Joh'es att Dene de Odyham qui obijt s. p.   Jacobus att=Amya vxor   Ricardus
Johana vxor ejus.                           Dene.   |   ejus.        atte Dene.

Elizabeth.   Amia.   Johannes att=Margeria filia   Misercecordia.   Christoferus &
                     Dene.   |   — Dunhurst.                        Jacobus s. p.
                                                                    —
                                                                    Ricardus.

Henricus Dene=Alicia f. Tho. Berington       Ricardus Dene.=Brigida filia Tho.
de Deneland. |  de Streightley.                          |   Berington.

Joh'nes   Jacobus   Will'mus.   Margareta.   Francisca.        Franciscus
Dene.     Dene.                 —            —                 Dene.
                                Alicia.      Elizabetha nupta
                                —            Steph'o Philip
                                Maria.       de Roffen.

# Searle.

ARMS. *Gules, on a chevron between three trefoils argent as many ogresses.*
CREST. *A demi-lion rampant or, holding a broken mast sable, the top set off with palisadoes, thereon a flag argent charged with a cross gules.*

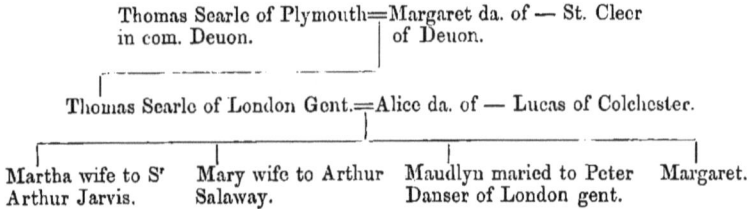

Thomas Searle of Plymouth=Margaret da. of — St. Cleer
in com. Deuon.    |    of Deuon.

Thomas Searle of London Gent.=Alice da. of — Lucas of Colchester.

| Martha wife to Sᵣ Arthur Jarvis. | Mary wife to Arthur Salaway. | Maudlyn maried to Peter Danser of London gent. | Margaret. |

# Naylour.

ARMS. *Or, a pale between two lions rampant sable.*
CREST. *A lion's head erased sable, charged on the neck with a saltire or.*

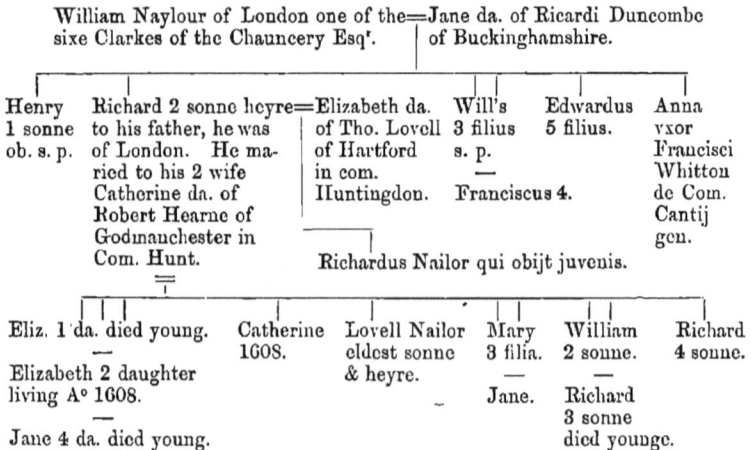

William Naylour of London one of the=Jane da. of Ricardi Duncombe
sixe Clarkes of the Chauncery Esqᵣ.    |    of Buckinghamshire.

| Henry 1 sonne ob. s. p. | Richard 2 sonne heyre to his father, he was of London. He maried to his 2 wife Catherine da. of Robert Hearne of Godmanchester in Com. Hunt. | =Elizabeth da. of Tho. Lovell of Hartford in com. Huntingdon. | Will's 3 filius s. p. — Franciscus 4. | Edwardus 5 filius. | Anna vxor Francisci Whitton de Com. Cantij gen. |

Richardus Nailor qui obijt juvenis.

| Eliz. 1 da. died young. — Elizabeth 2 daughter living Aº 1608. — Jane 4 da. died young. | Catherine 1608. | Lovell Nailor eldest sonne & heyre. | Mary 3 filia. — Jane. | William 2 sonne. — Richard 3 sonne died younge. | Richard 4 sonne. |

# Baron.

ARMS. *Azure, two lions passant guardant argent.*

Alice d. of — Harpesfeild his=Richard Baron Esq'=Margaret da. of — Morton
first wife. Citizen and Mercer his 2 wife.
ARMS. — *three harps or.* of London.

one sonne and a daughter.                    7 sonnes and 5 da.

# Weld.

ARMS. *Quarterly :—1 and 4. Azure, a fess nebulé between three crescents ermine. 2. . . . three lions rampant . . . a chief . . . 4. . . . three chevrons, each charged with a roundle . . .*

Richard Greswold of Solihull in com. Warr. Ar.=
ARMS. *Quarterly :—1 and 4. Argent, a fess gules between two greyhounds courant sable. 2 and 3. Argent, a chevron between three boars passant gules.* (STOKELEY.)

John Weld of Eaton in the= Roger Greswold of London=
County of Chester.          Marchantaylor 3 sonne.

John Weld of London=Dorothy onely daugh-=Hugh Offley Alderman of Lon-
2 sonne haberdasher. ter & heyre ob. 29 don 2 husband.
                     Junij A° 1610. ARMS. *Argent, a cross flory azure between four Cornish choughs proper.*

John Weld.   Elizabeth.   Joan.   Dorothy.          Susan.

# Cordell.

ARMS. *Gules, a chevron engrailed between three griffins' heads erased ermine.*
CREST. *A cockatrice, wings close vert, wattled beaked and collared or.*

Thomas Cordell of Enfeild in com. Midd.=

John Cordell of Enfeild.=          Robert Cordall.=

William Cordell of Fulham, Master   Thomas Cordell of
Cooke to Queene Elizabeth.          London, Mercer.

# Treswell.

ARMS. *Argent, three mullets pierced gules between two bendlets sable.*

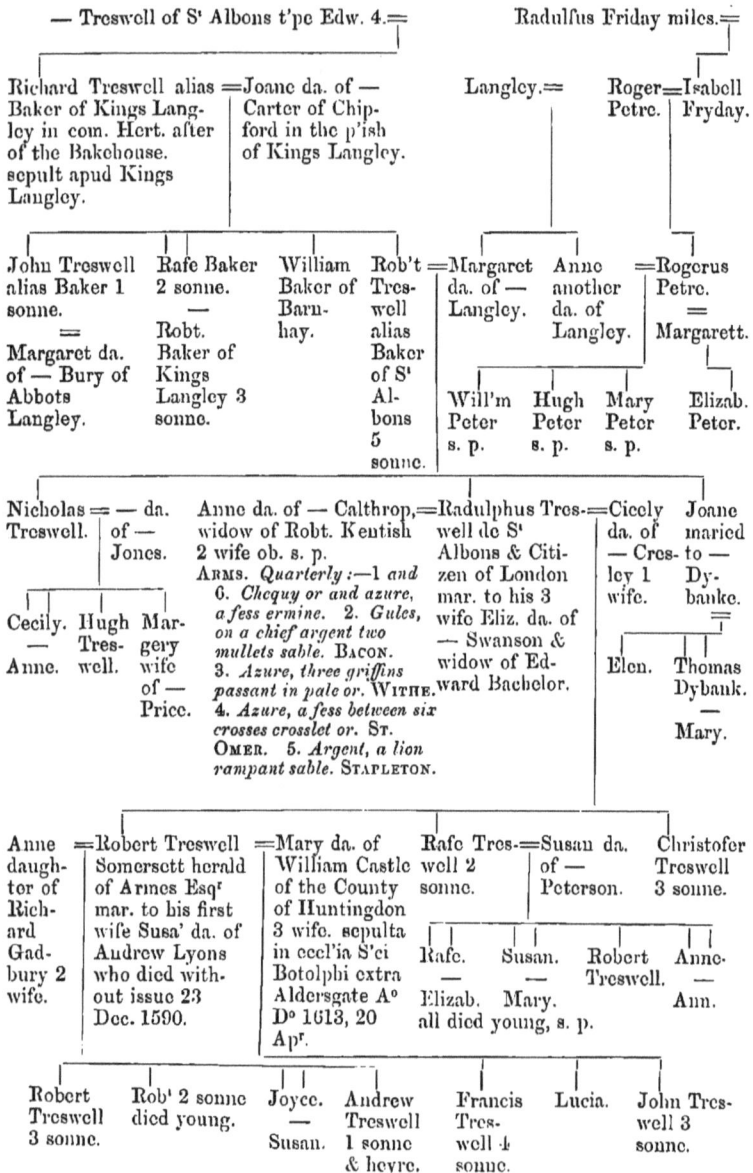

— Treswell of S' Albons t'pe Edw. 4.═

Radulfus Friday miles.═

Richard Treswell alias ═Joane da. of — Carter of Chipford in the p'ish of Kings Langley.
Baker of Kings Langley in com. Hert. after of the Bakehouse. sepult apud Kings Langley.

Langley.═

Roger═Isabell Petre. │ Fryday.

---

John Treswell alias Baker 1 sonne. ═ Margaret da. of — Bury of Abbots Langley.

Rafe Baker 2 sonne. — Robt. Baker of Kings Langley 3 sonne.

William Baker of Barnhay.

Rob't ═Margaret da. of — Langley.
well alias Baker of S' Albons 5 sonne.

Anne another da. of Langley.

═Rogerus Petre.
═
Margarett.

Will'm Peter s. p.

Hugh Peter s. p.

Mary Peter s. p.

Elizab. Peter.

---

Nicholas ═ — da. of — Jones.
Treswell.

Anne da. of — Calthrop, widow of Robt. Kentish 2 wife ob. s. p.
ARMS. *Quarterly:—1 and 6. Chequy or and azure, a fess ermine. 2. Gules, on a chief argent two mullets sable.* BACON. *3. Azure, three griffins passant in pale or.* WITHE. *4. Azure, a fess between six crosses crosslet or.* ST. OMER. *5. Argent, a lion rampant sable.* STAPLETON.

═Radulphus Treswell de S' Albons & Citizen of London mar. to his 3 wife Eliz. da. of — Swanson & widow of Edward Bachelor.

═Cicely da. of — Cresley 1 wife.

Joanne maried to — Dybanke.
═

Cecily. — Anne.

Hugh Treswell.

Margery wife of — Price.

Elen.

Thomas Dybank. — Mary.

---

Anne daughter of Richard Gadbury 2 wife.
═Robert Treswell Somersett herald of Armes Esq' mar. to his first wife Susa' da. of Andrew Lyons who died without issue 23 Dec. 1590.

═Mary da. of William Castle of the County of Huntingdon 3 wife. sepulta in eccl'ia S'ci Botolphi extra Aldersgate A° D° 1613, 20 Ap'.

Rafe Treswell 2 sonne.

═Susan da. of — Peterson.

Christofer Treswell 3 sonne.

Rafe. — Elizab.

Susan. — Mary.

Robert Treswell.

Anne. — Ann.

all died young, s. p.

---

Robert Treswell 3 sonne.

Rob' 2 sonne died young.

Joyce. — Susan.

Andrew Treswell 1 sonne & heyre.

Francis Treswell 4 sonne.

Lucia.

John Treswell 3 sonne.

# Freeman.

ARMS. *Azure, three lozenges argent, in chief a crescent or.*
CREST. *A demi-lion rampant (gules) charged with a lozenge (or).*

Martin Freeman of London=Elizabeth da. of Mathew Laurence; 2 sonne of
sonne of Edm. of Hanning- | S^r Oliuer Laurence.
ton in com. Northamp. | ARMS. *Quarterly:—1 and 4. Argent, a cross ragulé*
| *gules. 2 and 3. Argent, two bars and in chief*
| *three mullets gules.* WASHINGTON.

| Ralphe Freeman sonne and heyre ætatis 27 annor 1616. Lo. Mayor of London A° 1633. | Will'm 2 sonne. Martin 3 sonne. | John 4 sonne. Francis 5 sonne. | James 6 sonne. | Elizabeth wiffe of Stephen Haruey of London.= |

Martin æt 6 annor'.     Elizabeth 2 annor'.

# Le Maire.

ARMS. *Quarterly:—1. Argent, three moors' heads couped proper. 2. Gules, three boars' heads argent.* (BARY.) *3. Gules, a chevron between three lozenges argent. 4. Erminois, a crescent sable. 5. Argent, a bend lozengy gules, in chief an escallop azure. 6. Or, a martlet sable.*
CREST. *A moor's head couped proper, wreathed argent.*
MOTTO. *Tempera te tempori.*

Jacobus Le Maire=Catharina filia et hæres Petri de Bary de S^t Brixe ex Catha-
de Turnáy. | rina filia et hæres de Bonenfant.
| ARMS. *Quarterly:—1 and 6. Gules, three boars' heads argent. 2.*
| *Gules, a chevron between three lozenges argent. 3. Erminois, a*
| *crescent sable. 4. Argent, a bend lozengy gules, in chief an*
| *escallop azure. 5. Or, a martlet sable.*

David Le Maire=Sara filia Petri Trian de London.
de London. | ARMS. *Argent, a fess embattled between six estoiles or.*

| Henricus Swin-=Maria filia=Franciscus nerton de London prim' maritus. ARMS. *Quarterly:—1 and 4. Argent, a cross flory sable. 2 and 3. Argent, a cross flory sable within a bordure engrailed gules.* | prima Davidis le Maire. | Craue de Mortlack in com. Surr' miles 2 vx. ARMS. *Per bend or and azure.* | Petrus Le Maire de miles filius et hæres. | Edward Bacshe=Sara filia de Stansted in comitatu Hart- ford mil. ARMS. *Per chevron argent and gules, in chief two cocks sable, in base a saltire or.* Davidi Le Maire. |

# Baron.

ARMS. *Azure, two lions passant guardant argent.*
CREST. *Out of clouds argent a dexter arm in armour erect, couped at the elbow, holding in the gauntlet or a broken sword of the last, the blade proper.*

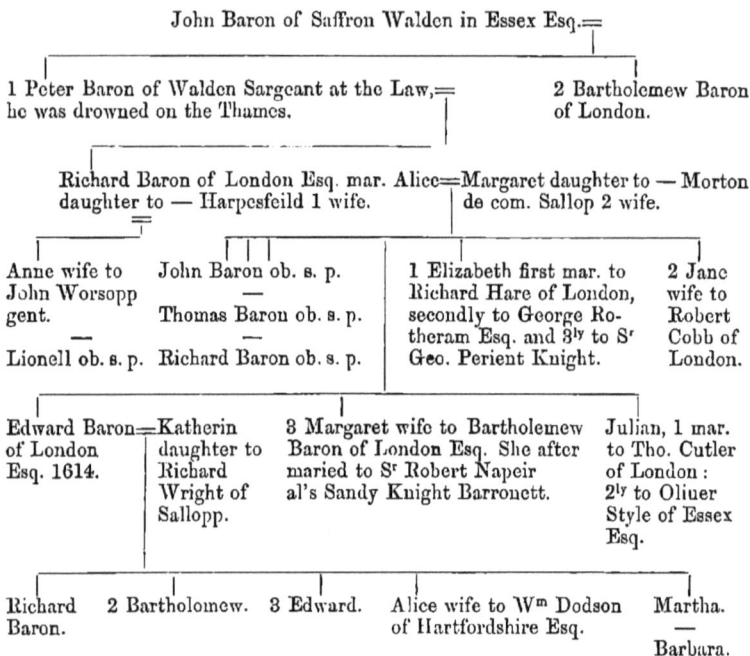

John Baron of Saffron Walden in Essex Esq.=

1 Peter Baron of Walden Sargeant at the Law,= he was drowned on the Thames.

2 Bartholemew Baron of London.

Richard Baron of London Esq. mar. Alice=Margaret daughter to — Morton daughter to — Harpesfeild 1 wife. de com. Sallop 2 wife.

Anne wife to John Worsopp gent.
—
Lionell ob. s. p.

John Baron ob. s. p.
—
Thomas Baron ob. s. p.
—
Richard Baron ob. s. p.

1 Elizabeth first mar. to Richard Hare of London, secondly to George Rotheram Esq. and 3ly to Sr Geo. Perient Knight.

2 Jane wife to Robert Cobb of London.

Edward Baron=Katherin of London Esq. 1614.
daughter to Richard Wright of Sallopp.

3 Margaret wife to Bartholemew Baron of London Esq. She after maried to Sr Robert Napeir al's Sandy Knight Barronett.

Julian, 1 mar. to Tho. Cutler of London : 2ly to Oliuer Style of Essex Esq.

Richard Baron.

2 Bartholomew.

3 Edward.

Alice wife to Wm Dodson of Hartfordshire Esq.

Martha.
—
Barbara.

# Dale.

ARMS. *Gules, on a mount vert a swan argent, membered and ducally gorged or.*
CREST. *On a chapeau . . . turned up ermine, a stork argent, beaked legged and ducally gorged or.*

This armes and creast was confirmed to William Dale of Brigstock and of London Ao 1613.

Robert Dale of Wencle in Prestbury in com. Chester.=Katherin daughter of —

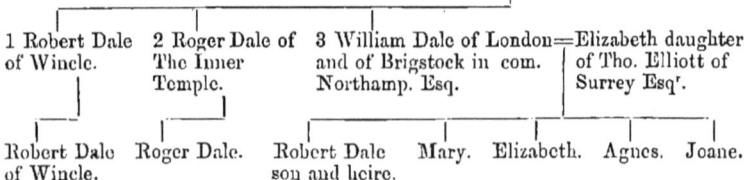

1 Robert Dale of Wincle.

2 Roger Dale of The Inner Temple.

3 William Dale of London=Elizabeth daughter and of Brigstock in com. of Tho. Elliott of Northamp. Esq. Surrey Esqr.

Robert Dale of Wincle.

Roger Dale.

Robert Dale son and heire.

Mary.

Elizabeth.

Agnes.

Joane.

# Morgan.

ARMS. *Quarterly :—1 and 4. Or, a fess wavy and in chief two eagles displayed sable.*
*2 and 3. Barry of twelve or and azure.* (COPCOTT.)
CREST. *An eagle displayed or, charged on the breast with a fess wavy sable.*

This Armes and Creast was confirmed by Mʳ William Dethick Garter A° 1588 to
Hugh Morgan, and sithence the same was confirmed by Mʳ Camden Clar. in
A° 1613 to Robert Morgan nephew & heire of the saied Hugh.

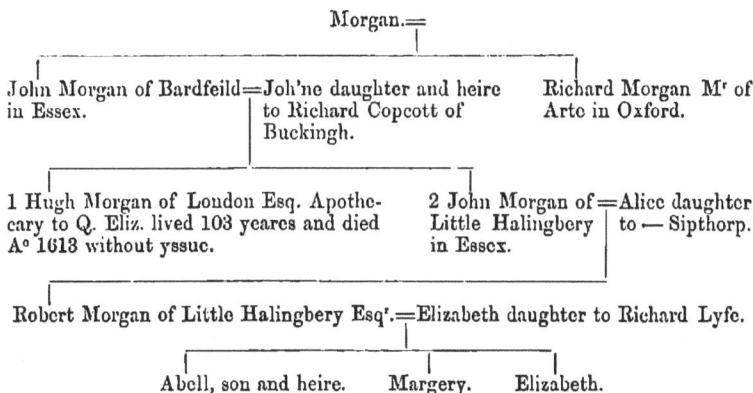

Morgan.=

John Morgan of Bardfeild=Joh'ne daughter and heire     Richard Morgan Mʳ of
in Essex.      to Richard Copcott of      Arte in Oxford.
     Buckingh.

1 Hugh Morgan of London Esq. Apothe-     2 John Morgan of=Alice daughter
cary to Q. Eliz. lived 103 yeares and died     Little Halingbery | to — Sipthorp.
A° 1613 without yssue.      in Essex.

Robert Morgan of Little Halingbery Esqʳ.=Elizabeth daughter to Richard Lyfe.

Abell, son and heire.     Margery.     Elizabeth.

# Gabott.

Robert Gabot of Acton Burnell in the County of Sallop had this Banner giuen=
him by Maximilian the Emperor for his Seruice (viz.)
*Gules, a griffin segreant or, holding in his claws a flagstaff bendy argent and sable, on
it a flag of the third charged with a double-headed eagle displayed of the second.*

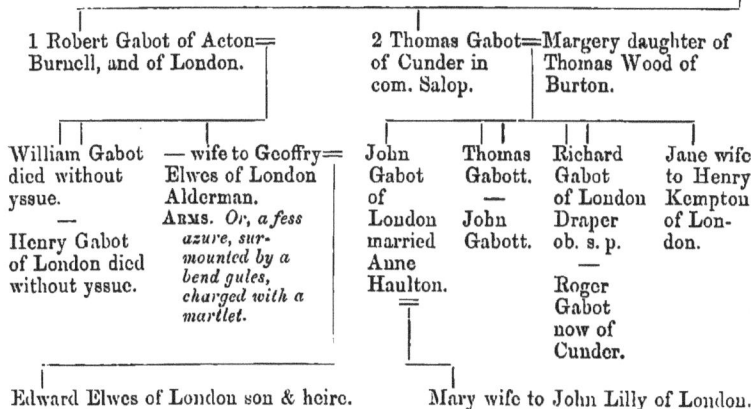

1 Robert Gabot of Acton=     2 Thomas Gabot=Margery daughter of
Burnell, and of London.      of Cunder in | Thomas Wood of
     com. Salop. | Burton.

William Gabot    — wife to Geoffry=   John    Thomas    Richard    Jane wife
died without    Elwes of London |   Gabot    Gabott.    Gabot    to Henry
yssue.    Alderman. |   of     —    of London   Kempton
—    ARMS. *Or, a fess*   London   John    Draper    of Lon-
Henry Gabot    *azure, sur-*   married   Gabott.   ob. s. p.    don.
of London died   *mounted by a*   Anne      —
without yssue.   *bend gules,*   Haulton.      Roger
   *charged with a*   =       Gabot
   *martlet.* |      now of
      Cunder.

Edward Elwes of London son & heire.     Mary wife to John Lilly of London.

## Allaunson of London.

ARMS. *Quarterly :*—1 *and* 4. *(Argent) a fess (azure) between three boars' heads couped (sable).* 2 *and* 3. . . . *three covered cups, two and one* . . . ; *over all a martlet for difference ; impaling (gules) a chevron ermine between three round buckles (or), in chief a mullet for difference.* (DALBY.)

CREST. *A pheon (argent), in it a broken staff-handle (or), charged with a martlet for difference. Another : A mule's head erased.*

Christopher Allaunson in yᵉ County=Jane daughter and heire of
Palatine of Durham. | Sʳ George Walkope.

Edward Allaunson of Huby=Joane da. of John Buckborow of Huby
in yᵉ County of York. | in yᵉ County of York.

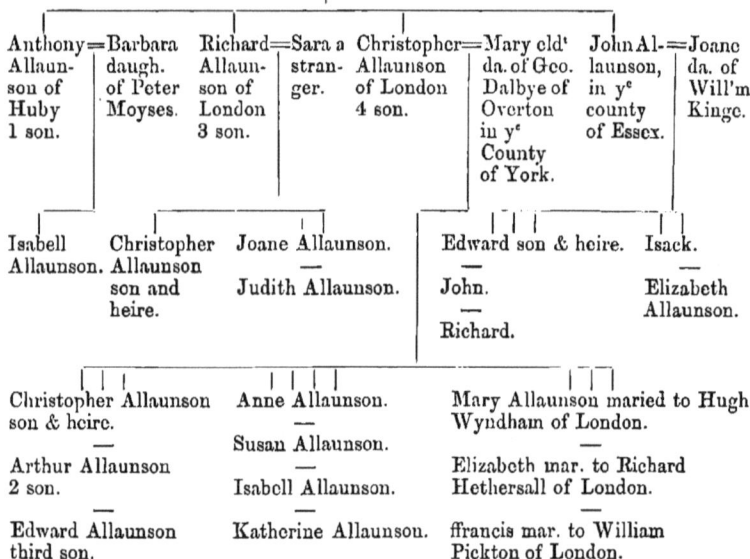

| Anthony=Barbara | Richard=Sara a | Christopher=Mary eld' | JohnAl-=Joane |
|---|---|---|---|
| Allaun- daugh. son of of Peter Huby Moyses. 1 son. | Allaun- stran- son of ger. London 3 son. | Allaunson da. of Geo. of London Dalbye of 4 son. Overton in yᵉ County of York. | launson, da. of in yᵉ Will'm county Kinge. of Essex. |

| Isabell Allaunson. | Christopher Allaunson son and heire. | Joane Allaunson. — Judith Allaunson. | Edward son & heire. — John. — Richard. | Isack. — Elizabeth Allaunson. |

Christopher Allaunson
son & heire.
—
Arthur Allaunson
2 son.
—
Edward Allaunson
third son.

Anne Allaunson.
—
Susan Allaunson.
—
Isabell Allaunson.
—
Katherine Allaunson.

Mary Allaunson maried to Hugh
Wyndham of London.
—
Elizabeth mar. to Richard
Hethersall of London.
—
ffrancis mar. to William
Pickton of London.

**Vernon of London** the blind Marchant Stapler who died Nouc'br 1616 since prole a great benefactour to the Marchant Tailors company.

ARMS. *Or, on a fess azure three garbs of the field, in chief two mullets gules.*
CREST. *A stag sejant or.*

**Ferrers of London** Lynnen draper.

ARMS. *Argent, on a bend gules cotised azure three horse-shoes or.*
CREST. *An ostrich proper, holding in the beak a horse-shoe or.*

### Sr John Ring of London.

ARMS. *Sable, a lion passant or, a label of three points argent.*
CREST. *On a ducal coronet a lion rampant or, holding in his paw a lance argent on the point thereof an annulet or.*

**Robynson of London** Cheif wayter of the Custome howse.

ARMS. *Vert, on a chevron between three stags statant or, as many trefoils gules; impaling Quarterly:—1 and 4. Sable, a chevron ermine between three rams' heads erased argent. 2 and 3. Argent, a lion rampant sable, surmounted by a fess engrailed gules.*
CREST. *A stag statant or, pelletté.*

### Gomersall of London.

ARMS. *Sable, a chevron engrailed ermine between three dexter gauntlets argent.*
CREST. *On a crescent or, a dexter gauntlet argent, grasping a battle-axe gules, pointed and headed of the second.*

Given by Sr Gilbt. Dethick Garter.

**Cooper of London** dwelling in Cornhill by the Exchange buried 13 of June 1609.

ARMS. *Argent, three martlets gules, on a chief engrailed of the second three annulets or, a crescent for difference; impaling sable, a fess dancetté argent, in chief two chaplets or.*

### Borlacy of London.

ARMS. *Quarterly:—1 and 4. Or, three pales sable, fretty of the field. 2 and 3. Gules, three castles argent, and as many lions issuing therefrom or.*
CREST. *A stag's head erased proper, holding in his mouth a ribbon with the motto, "SPES MEA DEVS," thereon.*

### Doctor Mountford of London the Phisicion.

ARMS. *Argent, three fleurs-de-lis gules, a martlet for difference; impaling gules, a chevron ermine between three garbs or.*

### William Thwaytes of London Alderman 1597.

ARMS. *Argent, a cross sable fretty of the field, in the first quarter a fleur-de-lis gules.*
CREST. *A gamecock proper, beaked and wattled gules, charged on the breast with a fleur-de-lis of the last.*

p' Wm Dethick Garter & Wm Camden Clarenc. 1597.

### Sr James Deane Knight of London.

ARMS. *Gules, a lion sejant guardant or, on a chief argent three crescents gules.*
CREST. *A demi-lion rampant, holding in his dexter paw a crescent.*

O

**Geffrey Elwes** Sherif of London, 1607.

ARMS. *Or, a fess azure, surmounted by a bend gules charged with a martlet argent.*
CREST. *Five arrows or, entwined by a snake vert.*

**Webling of London** Brewer, whose father was a Stranger.

ARMS. *Or, on a chevron sable a ram's head couped argent, on a chief of the second three lozenges or.*

**John Dent of London** and his wife daughter of — Graunt.

ARMS. *Sable, a fess indented argent, in chief three escallops or ; impaling gules, a vine-branch vert fructed argent, surmounted by a bend ermine.*
CREST. *A demi-wolf sable, charged on the neck with a collar dancetté argent.*

**Morison of London** since altered.

ARMS. *Per saltire or and gules, in pale two leopards' heads of the first, in fess two pelicans of the second, on a chief or, three chaplets gules.*
CREST. *A demi-pegasus or.*

**S**r **Tho. Fleming** Lo. Cheif Justice of England.

ARMS. *Gules, on a chevron between three owls (argent) an ermine spot sable.*

**S**r **Edw. Coke** Lo. Cheif Justice of the Comon Pleas.

ARMS. *Quarterly :—1. Per pale gules and azure, three eagles displayed argent.   2. Argent, a chevron azure between three chaplets gules.   3. Sable, a chevron . . . between three covered cups or.   4. Gules, semé of crosses crosslet fitché, a griffin segreant or.*

**S**r **Danyell Dun** one of the Masters of the requests.

ARMS. *Quarterly :—1 and 4.  Azure, a wolf salient and a chief argent.   2. Argent, a lion rampant gules, surmounted by a bendlet sable.   3. Gules, a fess vair, in chief an unicorn passant between two mullets or, a bordure engrailed of the last.*
WILKINSON.

**S**r **William Waade** Lieutenant of the Tower.

ARMS. *Quarterly :—1. Azure, a saltire between four escallops or.   2. Or, a chevron between three eagles' heads erased sable.   3. Gules, three garbs or.   4. Azure, two bars argent, on a chief of the last three maunches gules.*

**S**r **Thomas Edmonds** Clark of the Counsell.

ARMS. *Or, a chevron azure, on a canton of the second a fleur-de-lis of the field.*

**S**r **Thomas Lake** Clark of the Signett.

ARMS. *Quarterly :—1 and 4.  Sable, on a bend between six crosses crosslet fitché argent, a mullet of the field.   2 and 3. Quarterly argent and sable, on a bend gules three mullets argent, a martlet or for difference.*

**S**r **Thomas Smythe** Clarke of the Counsell.

ARMS. *Azure, a lion rampant or, on a chief argent three torteaux.*

**S**r **Julius Cesar** Chauncellor of the Exchequer.

ARMS. *Quarterly :—1 and 4.  Per fess argent and gules, six roses counterchanged.   2. Argent, two bars sable, on a chief of the last three swans argent.   3. Gules, three crescents argent.*

# INDEX OF NAMES.

A name in Italics signifies that the arms are blazoned.
" Capitals " there is a pedigree given.
" Brackets is the maiden name.
= signifies "married to a."

Mayte, —, 61.
*Meade*, 27.
Meade, Christopher, 84.
  Richard, 22.
  Thomas, 27.
*Merbury*, 51.
Merbury, Agnes (Blount), 51.
  William, 51.
Meredith, Philip, 64.
Merifeeld, —, 78.
*Merry*, 11.
Merslinge, —, 50.
*Metcalfe*, 42.
METCALFE, 42.
  Alice (Cook), 42.
  Anne = Elkyn, 42.
  Thomas, 42.
Michell, —, 87.
  —, 50.
Michenar, John, 51.
Midleton, Elena, 43.
  Elizabeth, 43.
  Anne (Anthony), 43.
  Richard, 43.
  Thomas, 43.
  William, 43.
  —, 54.
Mildmay, Sir Walter, 37.
Miller, John, 25.
  Nicholas, Sir, 85.
Mollyns, Sir Micheal, 39.
Montgomery, Sir John, 24.
Monyngs, Sir Edward, 85.
Moore, Nicholas, 38.
Mording, Miles, 86.
More, William, 6.
*Morison*, 98.
Morton, Mary = Baron, 91, 94.
*Morgan*, 95.
MORGAN, 95.
  Abell, 95.
  Alice (Sipthorpe), 95.
  Elizabeth (Lyfe), 95.
  Elizabeth, 95.
  Hugh, 95.
  Joh'ne (Copcott), 95.
  John, 95.
  Margory, 95.
  Richard, 95.
  Robert, 95.
Moseley, Micheal, 36.
*Mountford*, 97.
Mountford, Dr., 97.
Mowsdale, John, 29.
Moyses, Peter, 96.
Munday, Julian (Gadbury), 24.
  John, Sir, 24.
  Vincent, 24.
*Muschamp*, 41.
MUSCHAMP, 41.
  Catarine (Louday), 41.
  Christopher, 41.
  Edward, 41.
  Jane = Crymes.
  John, 41.
  Rafe, 41.
  Susan = Toppesfeild.
  Thomas, 41.
  William, 41.
  — (Harman), 41.

MUSCHAMP—*continued.*
  — (Nynnes), 41.
  — (Scott), 41.
Myldonnay, —, 37.
*Mylles*, 11.
MYLLES, 11.
  — (Merry), 11.
Nailor, Catherine, 90.
  Elizabeth, 90.
  Jane, 90.
  Lovell, 90.
  Mary, 90.
  Richard, 90.
  William, 90.
Nanton, Robert, 35.
Napeir, al's Sandy, 94.
  Robert, Sir, 94.
*Naylour*, 90.
NAYLOUR, 90.
  Anna = Whitton, 90.
  Catherine (Hearne), 90.
  Edward, 90.
  Elizabeth (Lovell).
  Henry, 90.
  Jane (Duncombe), 90.
  Richard, 90.
  William, 90.
Needham, George, 84.
Nelson, Lucia = Peacock, 80.
Nethermill, Julinus, 5.
Nevill, Sir Henry, 15.
*Newdigate*, 34.
Newdigate, John, 34.
Newman, Alice = Holme, 34.
  John, 34.
  — = Tasker, 34.
  —, 69.
*Nichells*, 64.
Nichells, John, 64.
Nicholas, Sir Ambrose, 36.
  John, 36.
*Nicolls*, 66.
NICOLLS, 66.
  Christian (Thomson), 66.
  Elizabeth (Cook), 66.
  Ellen (Holt), 66.
  John, 66.
  Mary = Garrard, 66.
Norris, —, 56.
Norton, Richard, 81.
Nowell, —, 58.
Nynnes, 41.
Odloy, Richard, 1.
Odyon, Thomas, 38.
*Offley*, 64, 91.
OFFLEY, 64.
  Henry, 64.
  Hugh, 91.
  Joane (Nichells), 64.
  Mary (Lowe), 76.
  Mary (White), 64.
  Robert, 76.
  Susan, 91.
  Thomas, 64, 76.
  Thomas, Sir, 1, 64.
  — (Cradoke), 64.
*Okeover*, 62.
OKEOVER, 62.
  Elizabeth (Babington), 62.
  Elizabeth, 62.

OKEOVER—*continued.*
  Philip, 62.
  Rafe, 62.
  Rowland, 62.
  Sara, 62.
  Sibill (White), 62.
  Susan, 62.
Okinhorne, Elizabeth, 61.
*Oliph*, 8.
OLIPH, 8.
  Anne, 8.
  Catherine, 8.,
  Elizabeth, 8.
  Joan, 8.
  Joan (Eves), 8.
  Joane = Leigh, 8.
  John.
  Malern.
  Olive.
*Osborne*, a. 15.
OSBORNE, 15.
  Edward, Sir, 15.
  — (Hewett), 15.
Osmond, Agnes, 92.
  Henry, 22.
  Hester, 22.
  Mary (Salkyns), 22.
Packer, —, 55.
Page, —, 30.
Pagott, Lord William, 19.
  Anne (Smyth), 81.
*Painell*, 20, 21, 22.
*Pakington*, 2, 7, 26, 72.
Pakington, Humfrey, 2, 7, 9, 26, 72.
  John, Sir, 2.
  John, 28, 80.
Pargitor, Anthony, 12.
*Park*, 78.
Park, Susan = Haydon, 78.
*Parker*, 47, 66.
PARKER, 47.
  John, 47, 66.
  Margery (Crosse), 47.
  Margery (Allen), 47.
  William, 47.
Parkyn, John, 63.
*Partridge*, 37.
PARTRIDGE, 37.
  Affabel, 37.
  Anne (Filders), 37.
  Ellen = Bartellett, 37.
  Margery (Gilbard), 37.
  Mary = Wadnall, 37.
  Thomas, 37.
Parvish, Anne, 74.
  Elizabeth = Trott, 74.
  Ellen, 74.
  Gabriel, 75.
  George, 74.
  Henry, 74.
  Mary, 74.
  Thomas, 74.
Patrick, Richard, 88.
*Pattenson*, 63.
PATTENSON, 63.
  Alice (Kede), 63.
  Brannus, 63.
  Christian, 63.
  Ellen (Chew), 63.
  John, 63.

Q 2

# INDEX OF PLACES OTHER THAN LONDON MENTIONED
## IN THIS VISITACION.

# FOREIGN PLACES MENTIONED IN THE VISITACION.

9

# WHEN THE *COUNTY ONLY* IS MENTIONED.

Bedfordshire, 70, 81, 84.
Buckinghamshire, 36, 90.
Cambridgeshire, 86.
Cheshire, 88.
Cornwall, 16, 70.
Cumberland, 59, 67.
Derbyshire, 10.
Devonshire, 26.
Durham, 96.
Essex, 4, 9, 10, 31, 43, 45, 46, 47, 57, 61, 74, 79, 94, 96.
Hampshire, 15, 40.
Herefordshire, 35, 40.
Hertfordshire, 17, 36, 61, 84, 87.

Huntingdonshire, 58, 75, 92.
Isle of Wight, 6, 57.
Kent, 5, 22, 38, 45, 50, 53, 73, 82, 90.
Lancashire, 47, 59.
Leicestershire, 33, 71.
Lincolnshire, 11, 21, 23, 24, 26, 43, 66, 75, 87.
Monmouthshire, 87.
Norfolk, 13.
Northamptonshire, 15, 17, 30, 32.
Northumberland, 23, 53.
Oxfordshire, 8.

Shropshire, 4, 25, 28, 35, 39, 70, 94.
Somersetshire, 11, 39, 44.
Staffordshire, 10, 13, 20, 43, 68, 87.
Suffolk, 22, 27, 68.
Surrey, 56.
Sussex, 23, 37, 39, 72, 84, 88.
Warwickshire, 39, 47, 58, 83, 84, 87.
Wiltshire, 21, 68.
Worcestershire, 3, 34.
Yorkshire, 6, 15, 17, 23, 31, 46, 50, 64, 72, 76, 81, 96.

TAYLOR AND CO., PRINTERS,
LITTLE QUEEN STREET, LINCOLN'S INN FIELDS.

www.ingramcontent.com/pod-product-compliance
Lightning Source LLC
Chambersburg PA
CBHW031440280326
41927CB00038B/1247